Disney · PIXAR

TOKYOPOP®

Hamburg · London · Los

S0-DTC-070

Editors - Elizabeth Hurchalla and Zachary Rau
Graphic Designer and Letterer - Tomás Montalvo-Lagos
Cover Designer - Tomás Montalvo-Lagos

Digital Imaging Manager - Chris Buford
Production Manager - Elisabeth Brizzi
Senior Designer - Christian Lownds
Senior Editor - Elizabeth Hurchalla
Managing Editor - Lindsey Johnston
VP of Production - Ron Klamert
Publisher & Editor in Chief - Mike Kiley
President & C.O.O. - John Parker
C.E.O. - Stuart Levy

E-mail: info@TOKYOPOP.com
Come visit us online at
www.TOKYOPOP.com

A TOKYOPOP Cine-Manga® Book
TOKYOPOP Inc.
5900 Wilshire Blvd.,
Suite 2000
Los Angeles, CA 90036

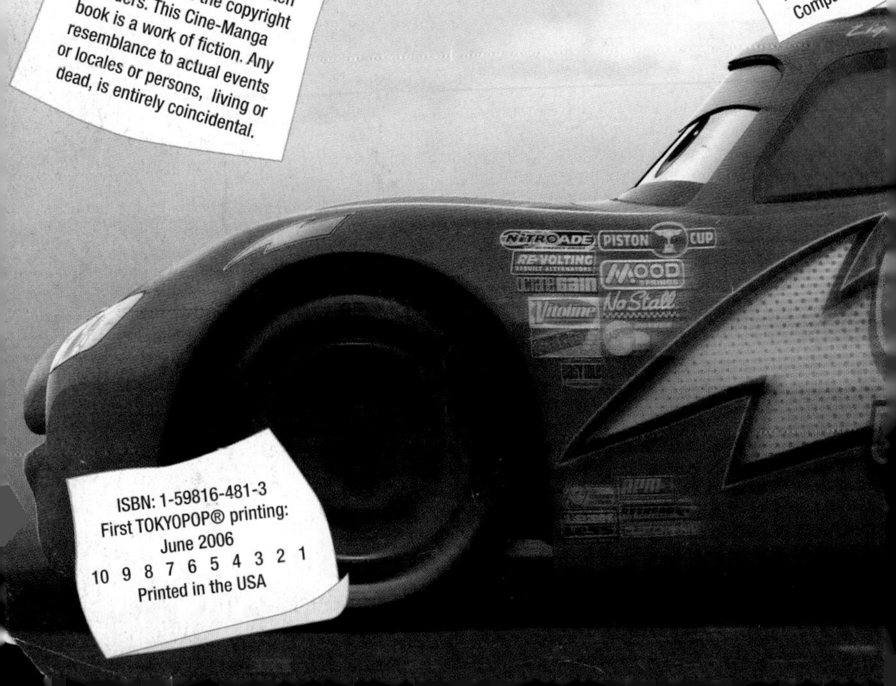
NITROADE
PISTON CUP
RE-VOLTING
No Stall

ISBN: 1-59816-481-3
First TOKYOPOP® printing: June 2006
10 9 8 7 6 5 4 3 2 1
Printed in the USA

Disney · PIXAR

Cars

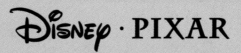

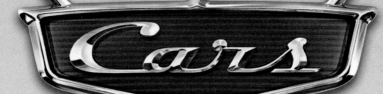

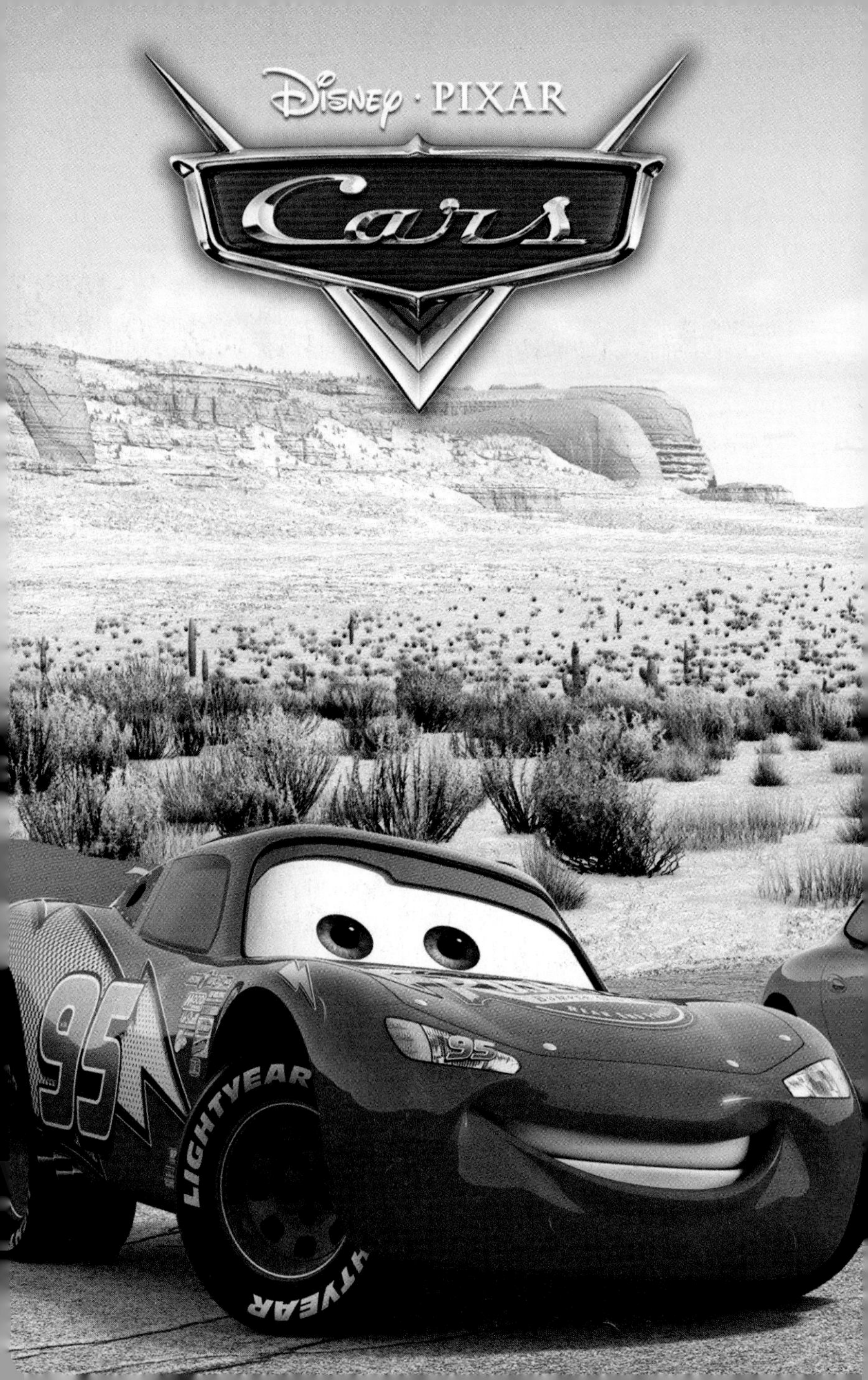
Disney · PIXAR
Cars
95
LIGHTYEAR

─Contents─

The Cast of

DISNEY · PIXAR

Cars

Lightning McQueen

McQueen is a hotshot rookie race car on the Piston Cup series. He has made a name for himself with his amazing driving and is tied with The King and Chick Hicks for first place going into the last race of the year. His eye is on the prize, and nothing else matters.

Chick Hicks

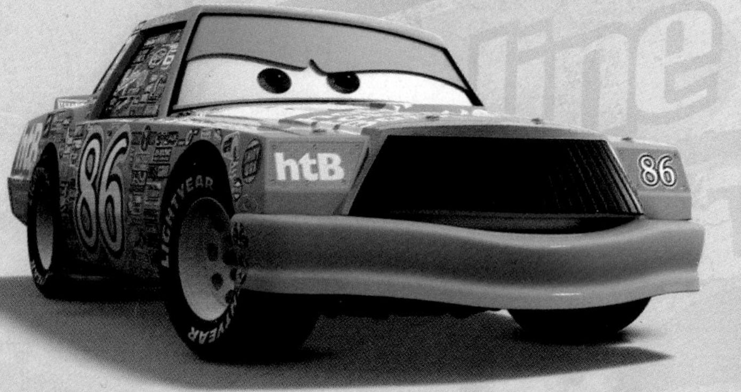
htB
86
LIGHTYEAR

A veteran on the Piston Cup circuit, he has always finished second to The King and has a big chip on his shoulder because of it. All Chick wants in life is to win the Piston Cup and get the coveted Dinoco sponsorship—and he will stop at nothing to get them. He hates McQueen for stealing his thunder.

Strip "The King" Weathers

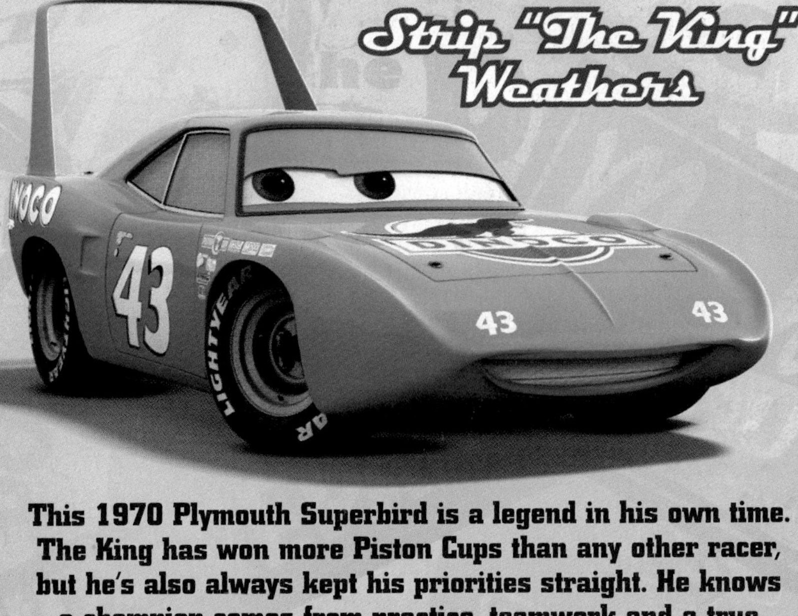
43
LIGHTYEAR

This 1970 Plymouth Superbird is a legend in his own time. The King has won more Piston Cups than any other racer, but he's also always kept his priorities straight. He knows a champion comes from practice, teamwork and a true heart. He just wants to win one last Cup before he retires.

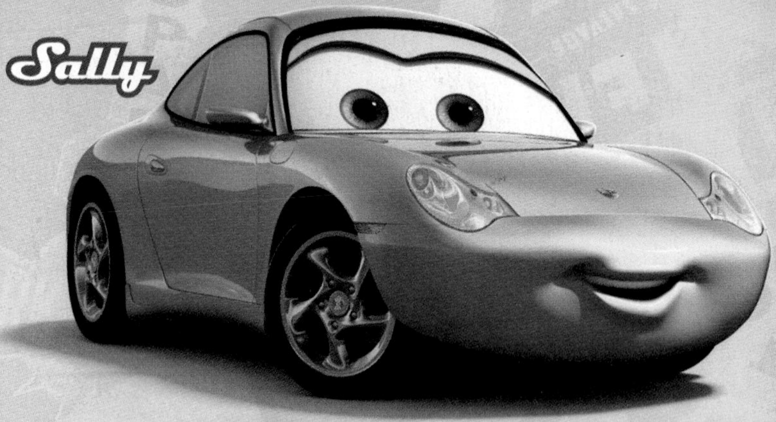
Sally

A Porsche 911, Sally lost her appetite for life in the California fast lane and found the speed of Radiator Springs much more to her liking. Her goal is to put Radiator Springs back on the map.

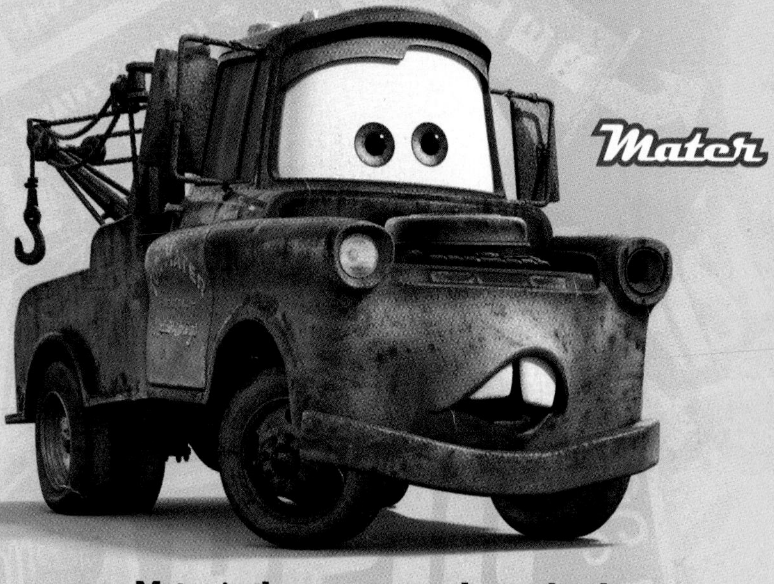
Mater

Mater is the sweetest and most loyal guy in Radiator Springs and the first to see McQueen for who he really is. A good-ol'-boy tow truck with a big heart, Mater loves tractor-tipping.

Doc Hudson

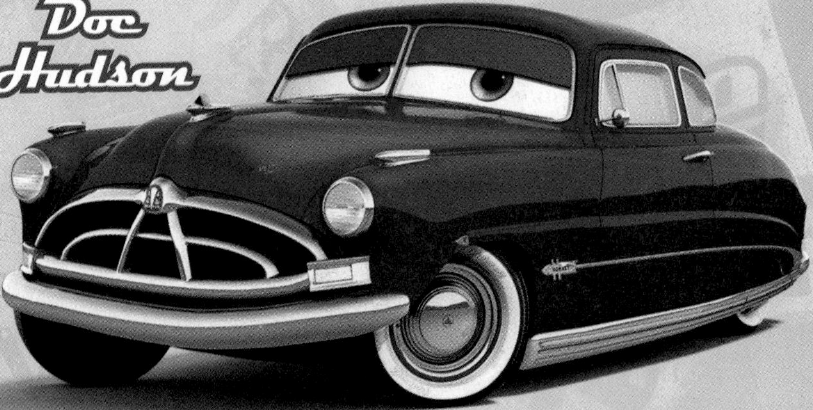

A 1951 Hudson Hornet, Doc Hudson is the town doctor and the town judge. He looks out for the townsfolk and their best interests. He is the heart of Radiator Springs with a mysterious past he is trying escape.

Sheriff

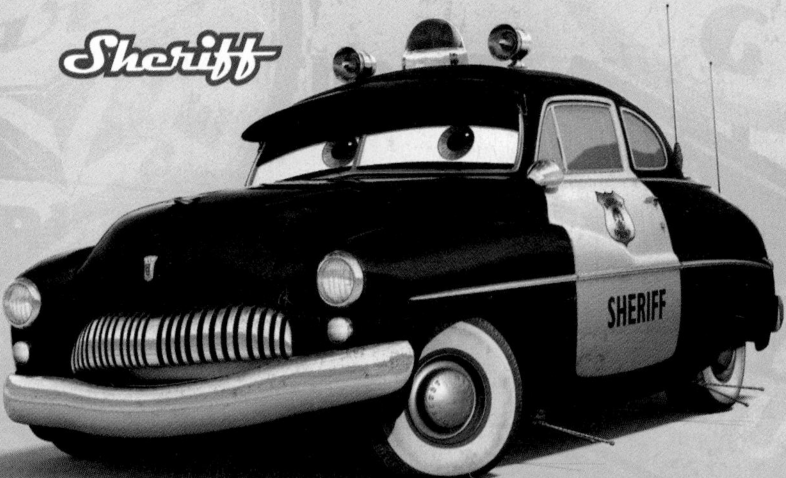
SHERIFF

The law in Radiator Springs is a 1949 Mercury police cruiser. Though Sheriff may eat a few too many doughnuts, he still takes his job seriously and is ready to catch anyone speeding through town.

Sarge

This surly 1942 WWII Willys Army Jeep is the owner of the local army surplus store and an extremely patriotic veteran. He can often be found arguing with his neighbor Fillmore.

Fillmore

Fillmore is a 1960 VW Bus that is stuck in the '60s. He brews his own organic fuel, which he sells from the tie-dyed dome he lives in. He drives Sarge nuts with his conspiracy theories and his hippie ways.

Luigi

Luigi is a 1959 Fiat 500 who owns the local tire shop, Luigi's Casa Della Tires, "Home of the Leaning Tower of Tires." He is an avid fan of Ferraris.

Guido

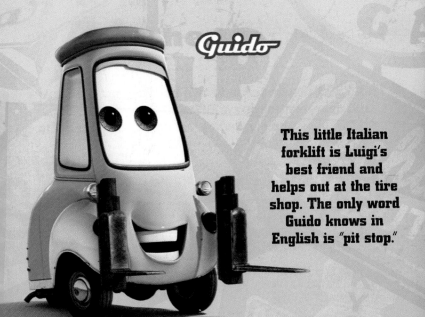

This little Italian forklift is Luigi's best friend and helps out at the tire shop. The only word Guido knows in English is "pit stop."

Flo

Flo is a 1950s show car who was passing through Radiator Springs on tour when she saw Ramone. It was love at first sight and she has never left. She runs the local diner, Flo's V8 Café, serving the finest fuel in fifty states.

Ramone

This 1959 Impala is the town's resident artist. He owns and operates Ramone's House of Body Art, the local custom body and paint shop. He only has eyes for Flo.

Red

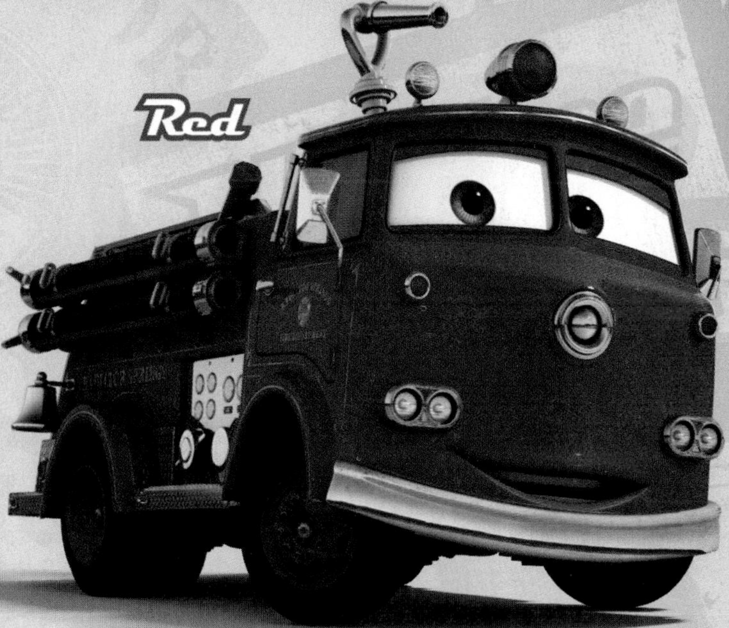

Though Red might not say much, he is always ready to help his neighbors if anyone needs it. He spends his days nurturing the flowers he plants around town.

Lizzie

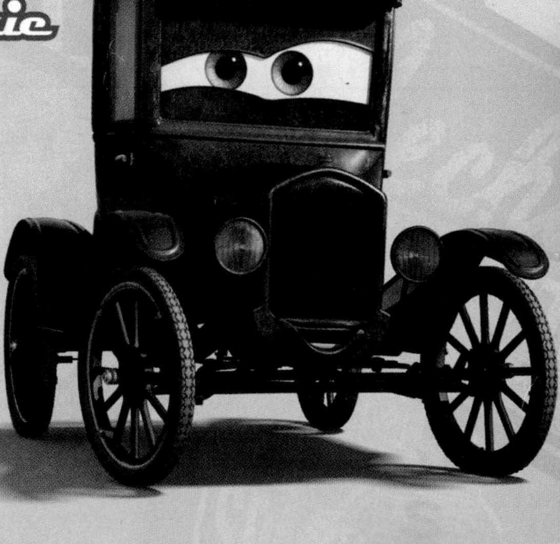

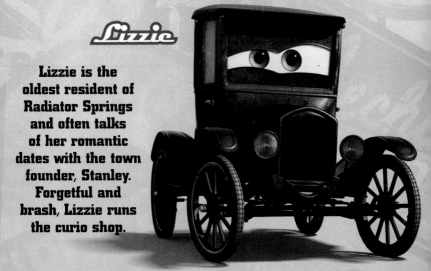

Lizzie is the oldest resident of Radiator Springs and often talks of her romantic dates with the town founder, Stanley. Forgetful and brash, Lizzie runs the curio shop.

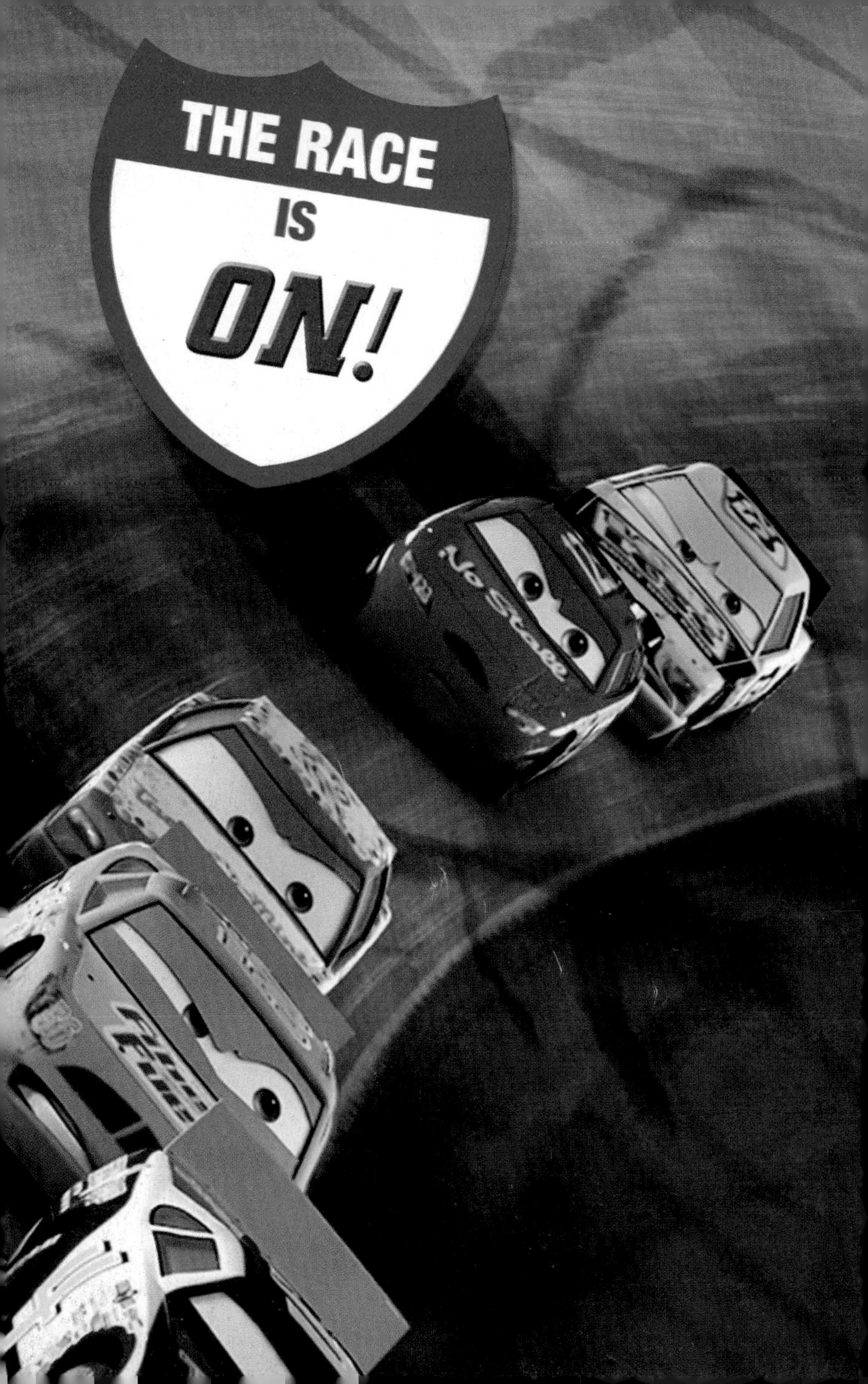
THE RACE
IS
ON!

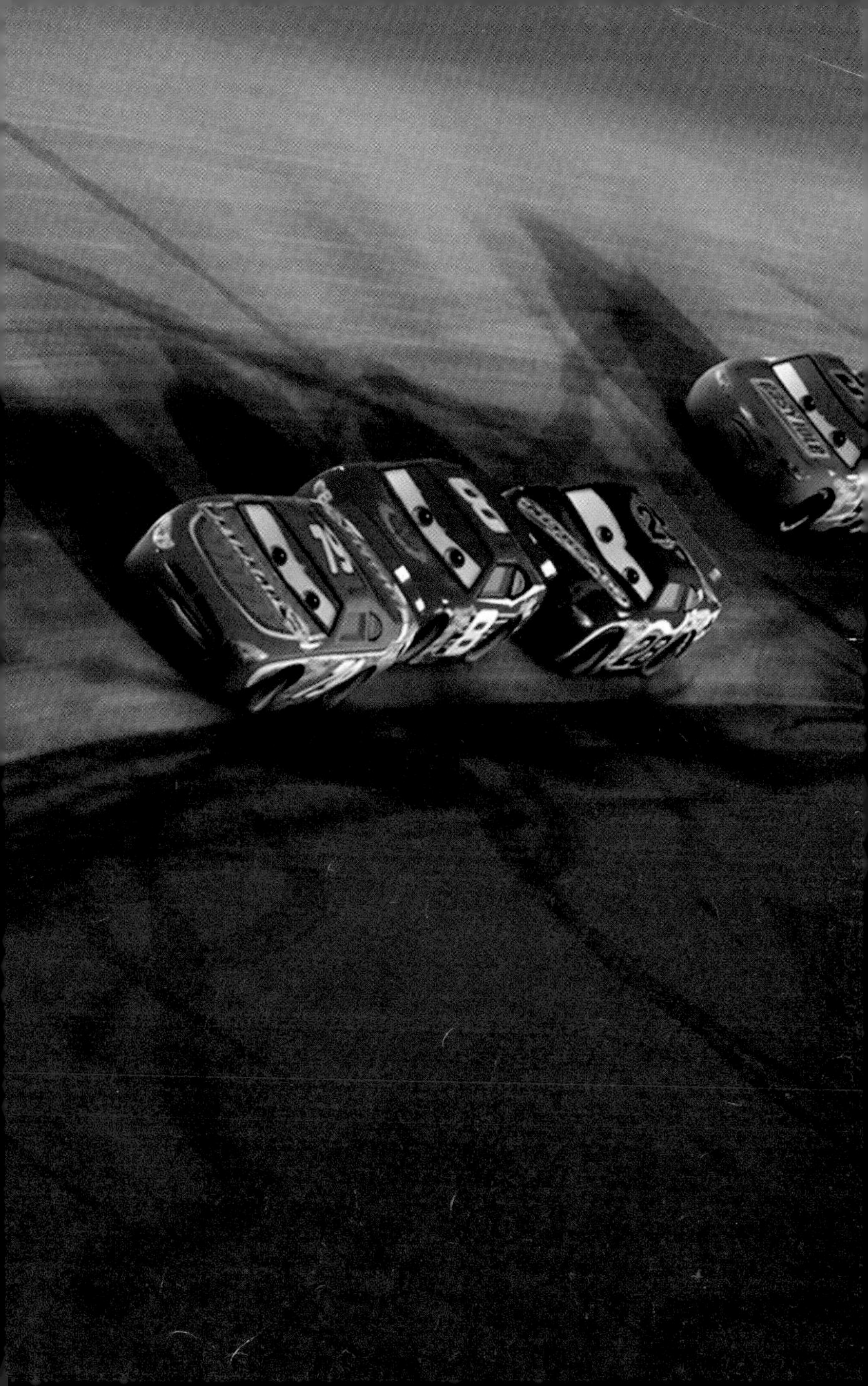

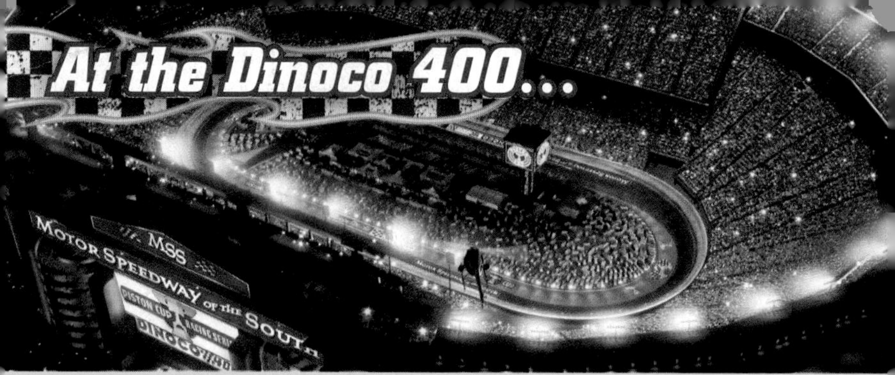
At the Dinoco 400...
MSS
MOTOR SPEEDWAY OF THE SOUTH
PISTON CUP

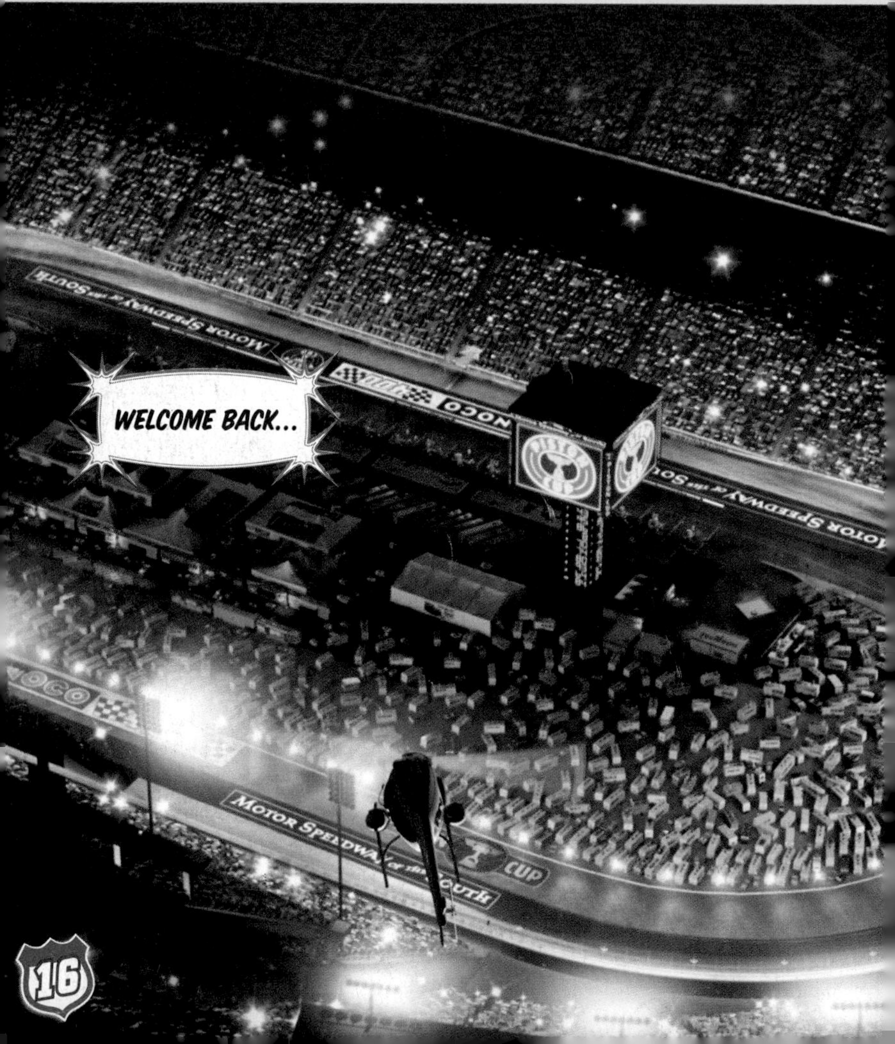
WELCOME BACK...
MOTOR SPEEDWAY of the SOUTH

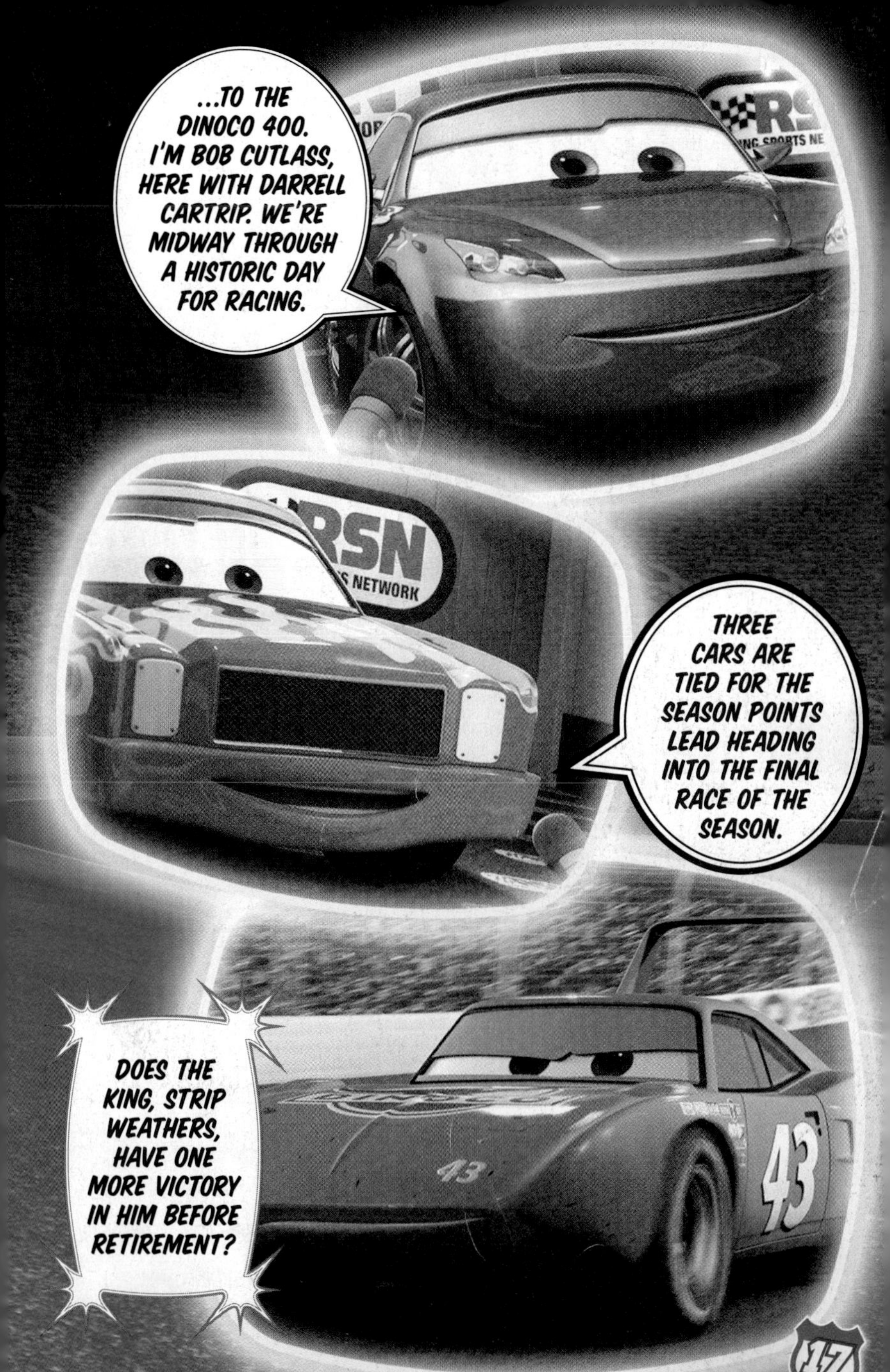
...TO THE DINOCO 400. I'M BOB CUTLASS, HERE WITH DARRELL CARTRIP. WE'RE MIDWAY THROUGH A HISTORIC DAY FOR RACING.
THREE CARS ARE TIED FOR THE SEASON POINTS LEAD HEADING INTO THE FINAL RACE OF THE SEASON.
DOES THE KING, STRIP WEATHERS, HAVE ONE MORE VICTORY IN HIM BEFORE RETIREMENT?

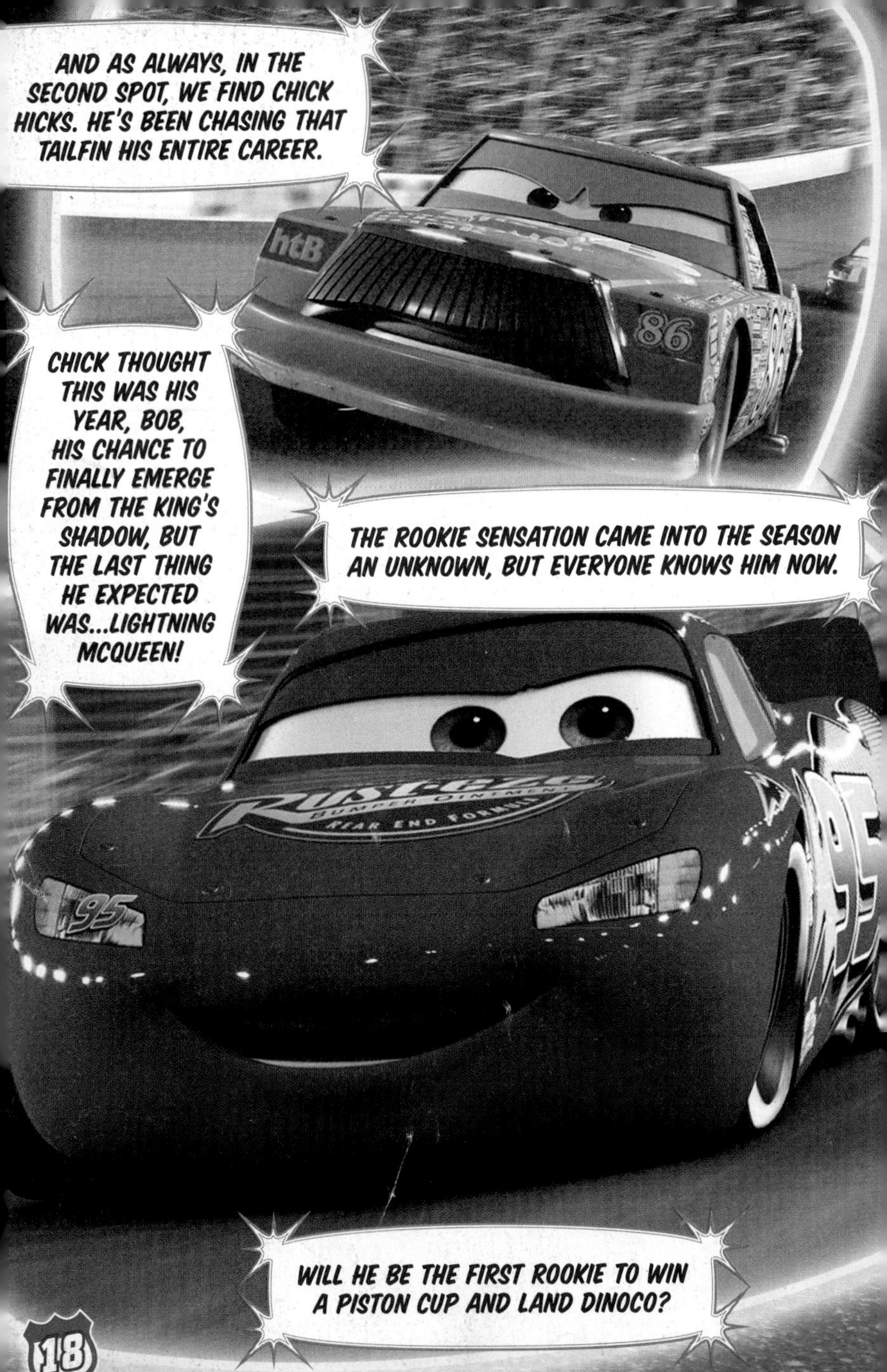
AND AS ALWAYS, IN THE SECOND SPOT, WE FIND CHICK HICKS. HE'S BEEN CHASING THAT TAILFIN HIS ENTIRE CAREER.
htB
86
CHICK THOUGHT THIS WAS HIS YEAR, BOB, HIS CHANCE TO FINALLY EMERGE FROM THE KING'S SHADOW, BUT THE LAST THING HE EXPECTED WAS...LIGHTNING MCQUEEN!
THE ROOKIE SENSATION CAME INTO THE SEASON AN UNKNOWN, BUT EVERYONE KNOWS HIM NOW.
REAR END FORMULA
95
WILL HE BE THE FIRST ROOKIE TO WIN A PISTON CUP AND LAND DINOCO?

As the laps tick by and Lightning McQueen attempts to take the lead, Chick Hicks slams him into the wall...

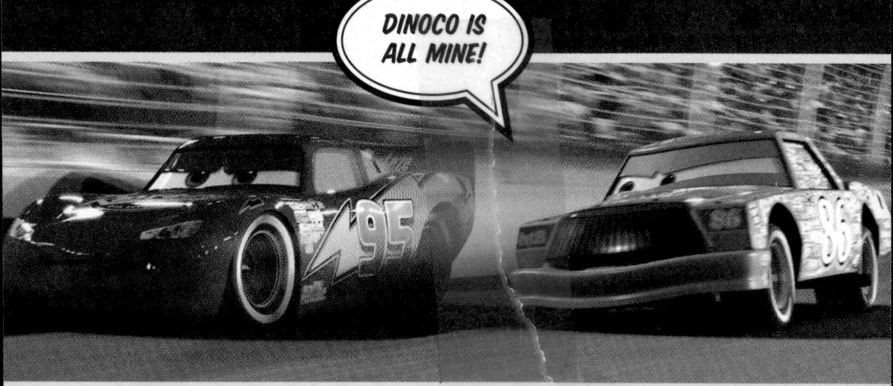
DINOCO IS ALL MINE!
95
86

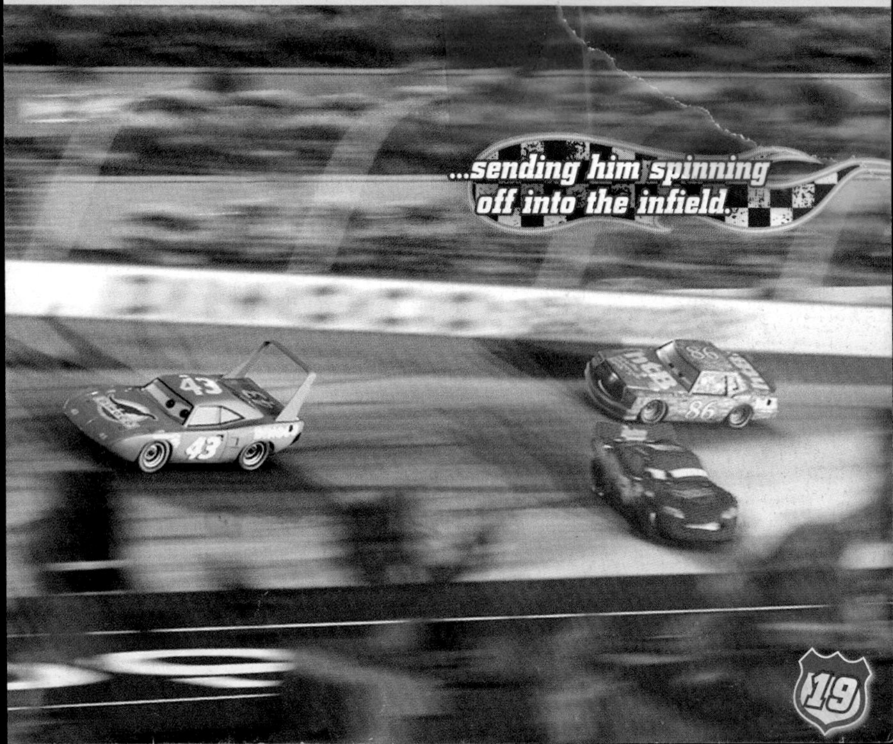
...sending him spinning off into the infield.
43
86

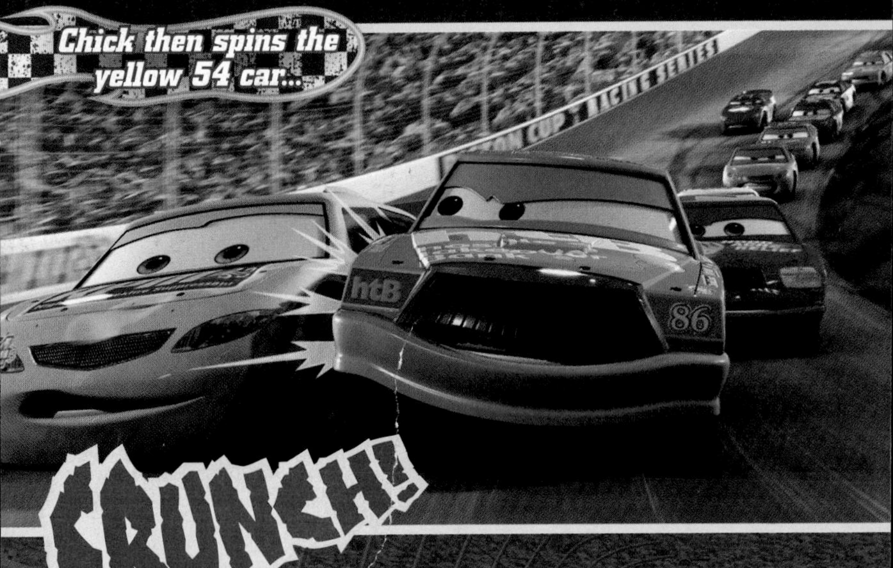
Chick then spins the yellow 54 car...
CRUNCH!

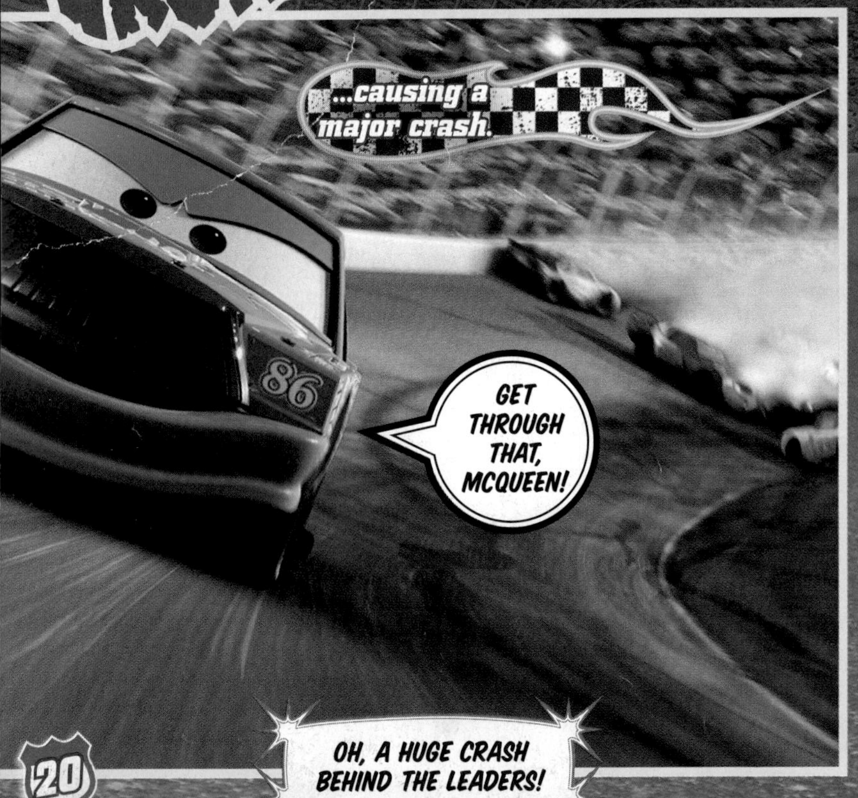
...causing a major crash.
GET THROUGH THAT, MCQUEEN!
OH, A HUGE CRASH BEHIND THE LEADERS!

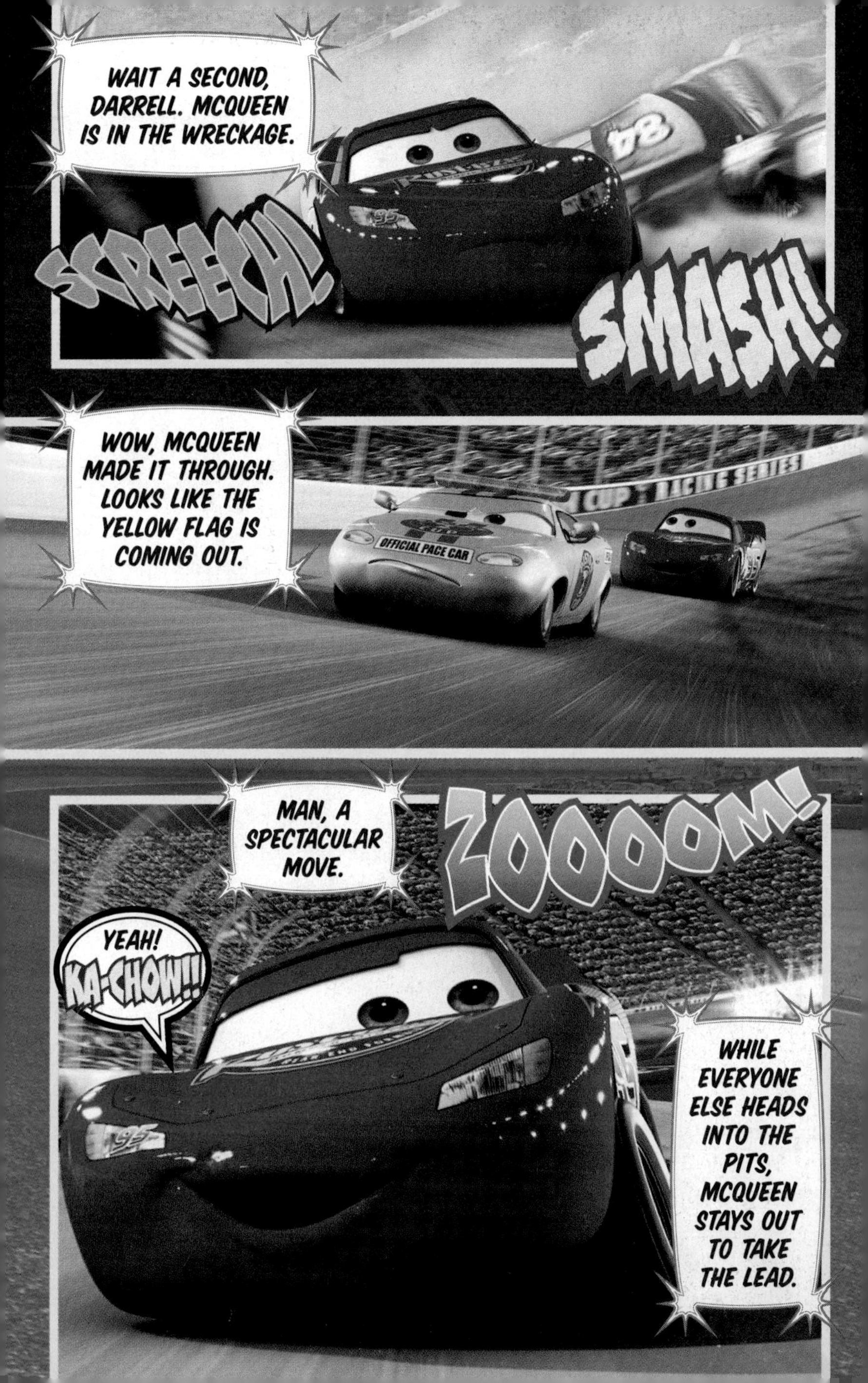
WAIT A SECOND, DARRELL. MCQUEEN IS IN THE WRECKAGE.
SCREECH!
SMASH!
WOW, MCQUEEN MADE IT THROUGH. LOOKS LIKE THE YELLOW FLAG IS COMING OUT.
OFFICIAL PACE CAR
MAN, A SPECTACULAR MOVE.
ZOOOOM!
YEAH! KA-CHOW!!!
WHILE EVERYONE ELSE HEADS INTO THE PITS, MCQUEEN STAYS OUT TO TAKE THE LEAD.

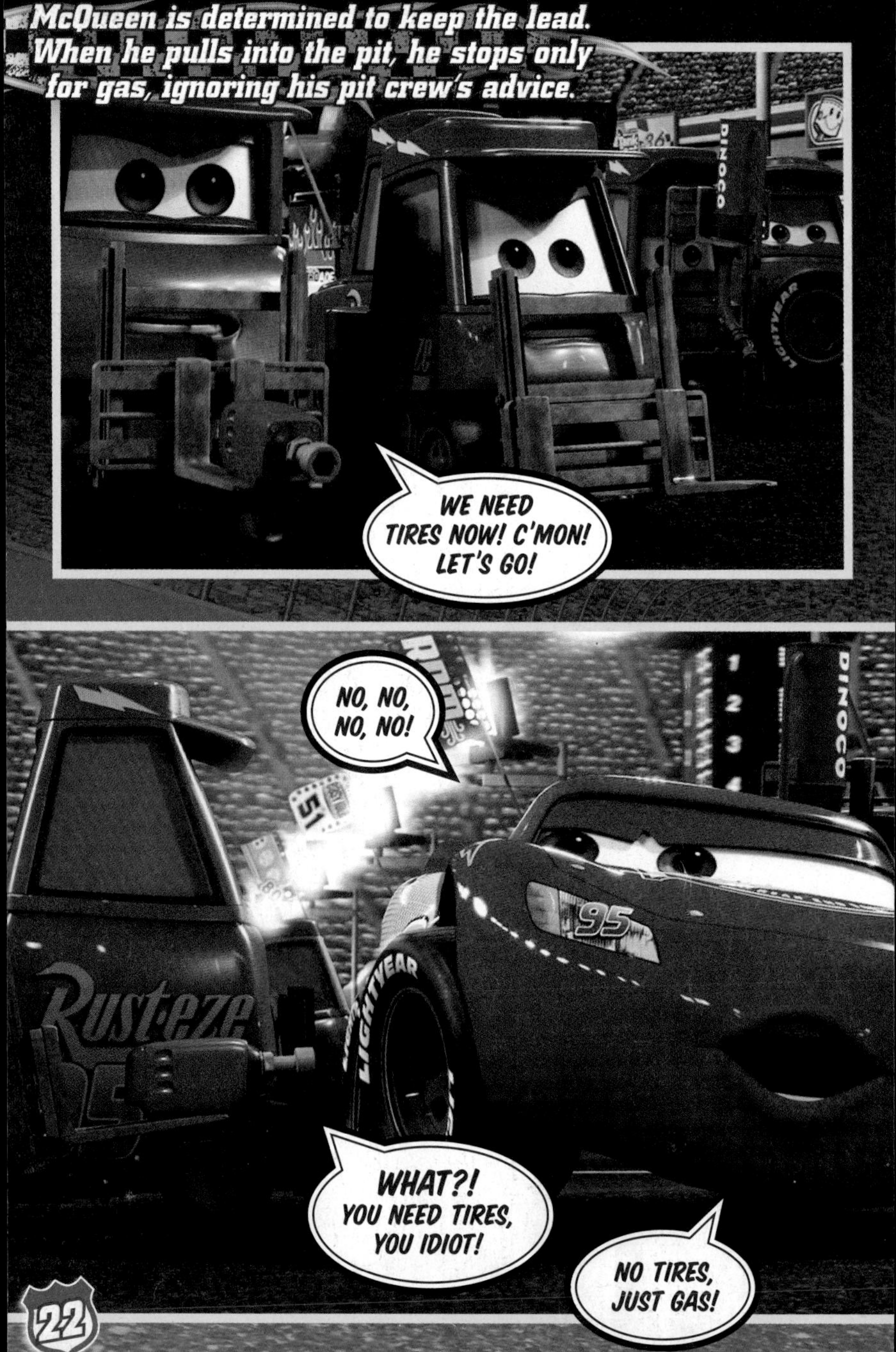
McQueen is determined to keep the lead. When he pulls into the pit, he stops only for gas, ignoring his pit crew's advice.
WE NEED TIRES NOW! C'MON! LET'S GO!
NO, NO, NO, NO!
WHAT?! YOU NEED TIRES, YOU IDIOT!
NO TIRES, JUST GAS!

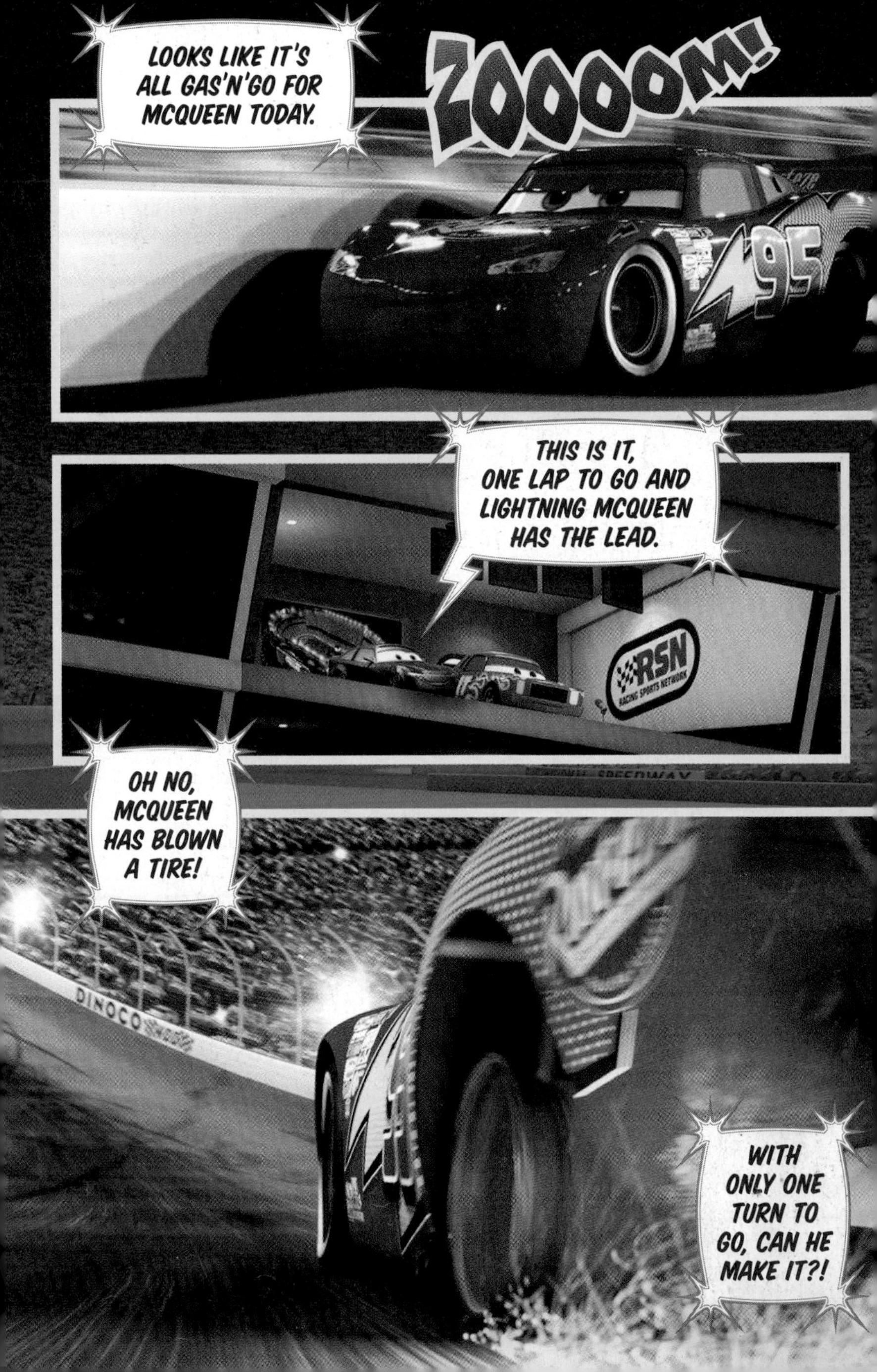
LOOKS LIKE IT'S ALL GAS'N'GO FOR MCQUEEN TODAY.
ZOOOOM!
95
THIS IS IT, ONE LAP TO GO AND LIGHTNING MCQUEEN HAS THE LEAD.
RSN
RACING SPORTS NETWORK
OH NO, MCQUEEN HAS BLOWN A TIRE!
DINOCO
WITH ONLY ONE TURN TO GO, CAN HE MAKE IT?!

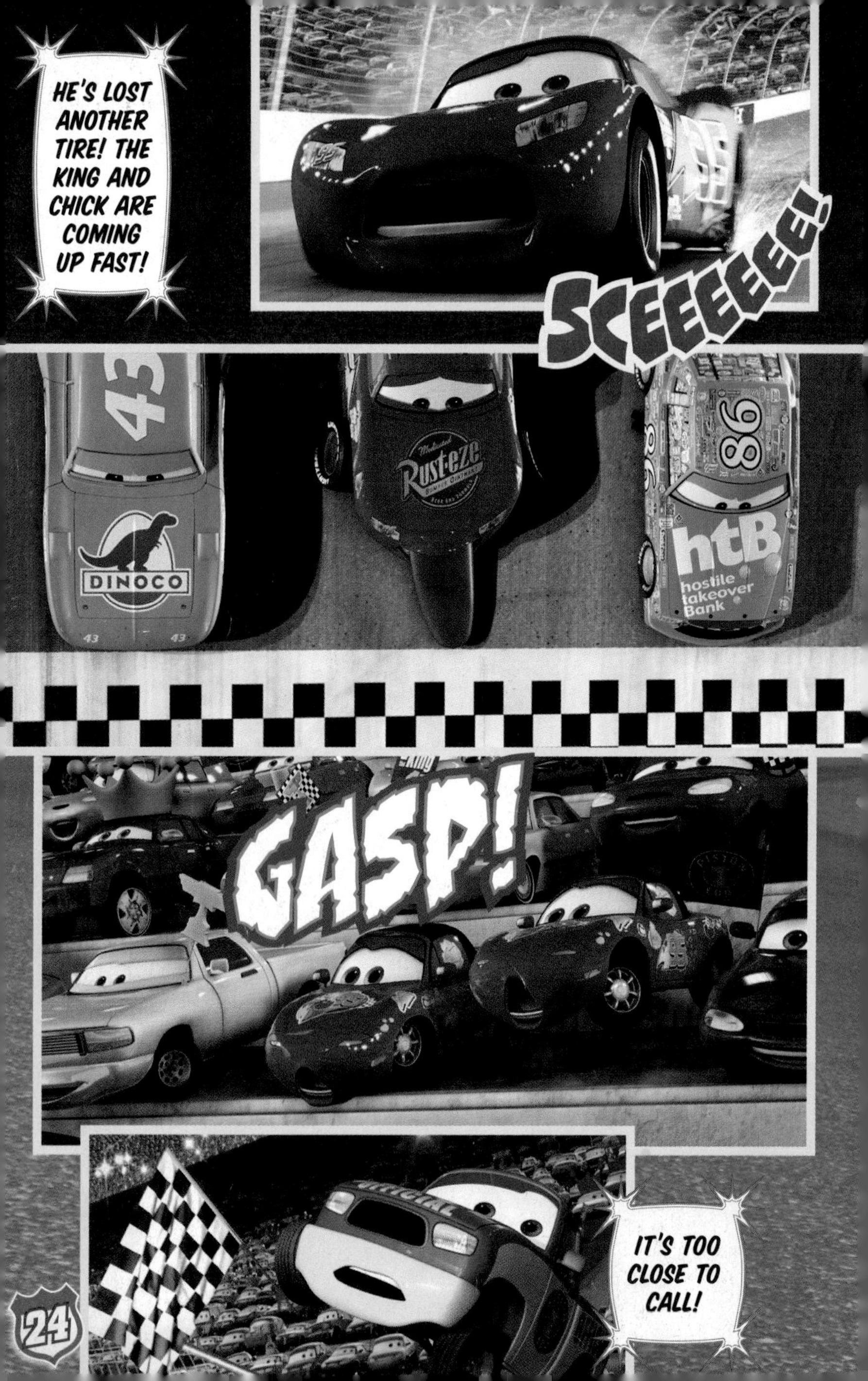
HE'S LOST ANOTHER TIRE! THE KING AND CHICK ARE COMING UP FAST!
SCEEEEEE!
43
DINOCO
Rust-eze
86
htB
hostile takeover Bank
GASP!
IT'S TOO CLOSE TO CALL!

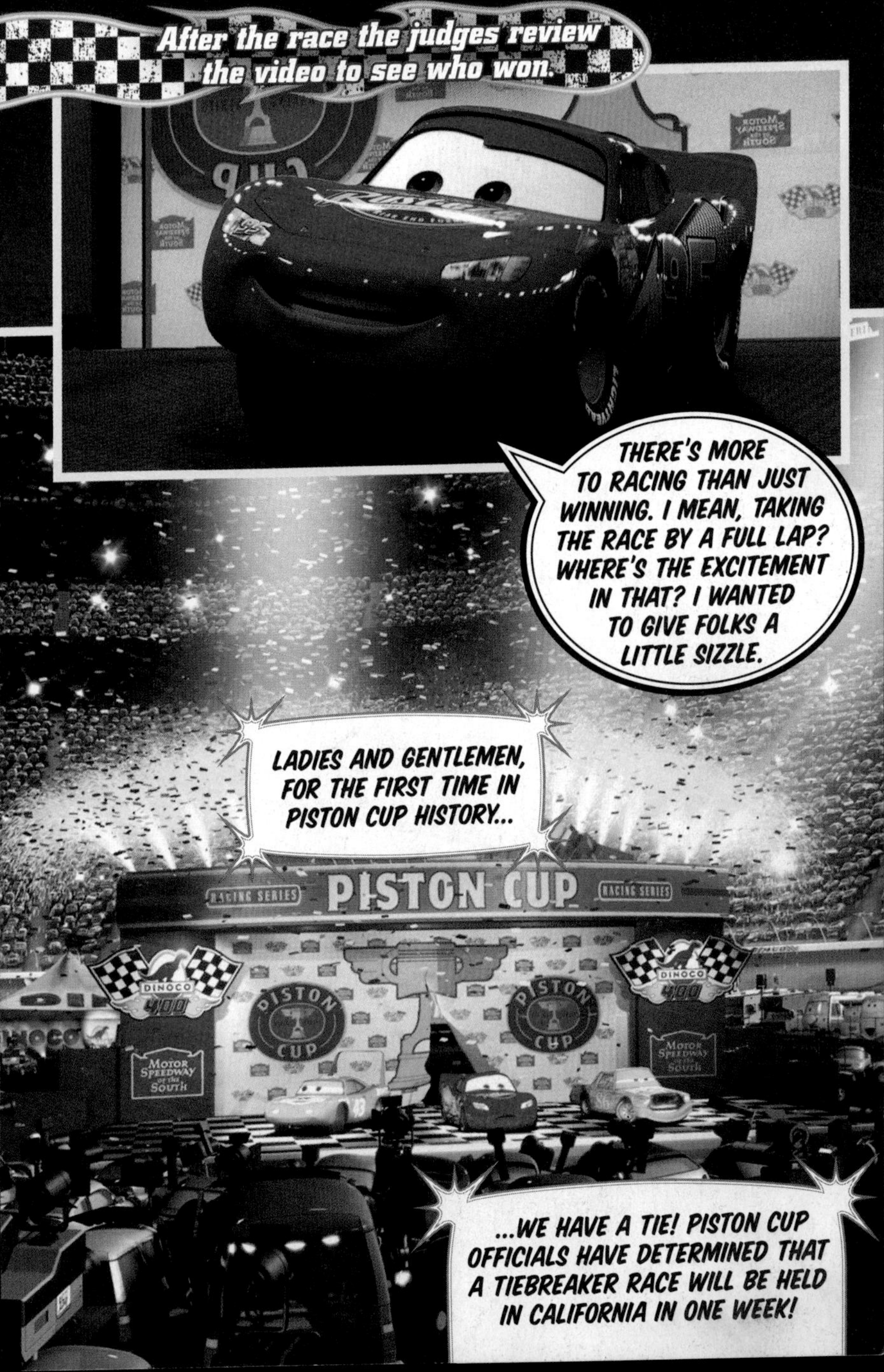

After the race the judges review the video to see who won.
THERE'S MORE TO RACING THAN JUST WINNING. I MEAN, TAKING THE RACE BY A FULL LAP? WHERE'S THE EXCITEMENT IN THAT? I WANTED TO GIVE FOLKS A LITTLE SIZZLE.
LADIES AND GENTLEMEN, FOR THE FIRST TIME IN PISTON CUP HISTORY...
PISTON CUP
RACING SERIES
RACING SERIES
DINOCO 400
DINOCO 400
PISTON CUP
PISTON CUP
MOTOR SPEEDWAY OF THE SOUTH
MOTOR SPEEDWAY OF THE SOUTH
...WE HAVE A TIE! PISTON CUP OFFICIALS HAVE DETERMINED THAT A TIEBREAKER RACE WILL BE HELD IN CALIFORNIA IN ONE WEEK!

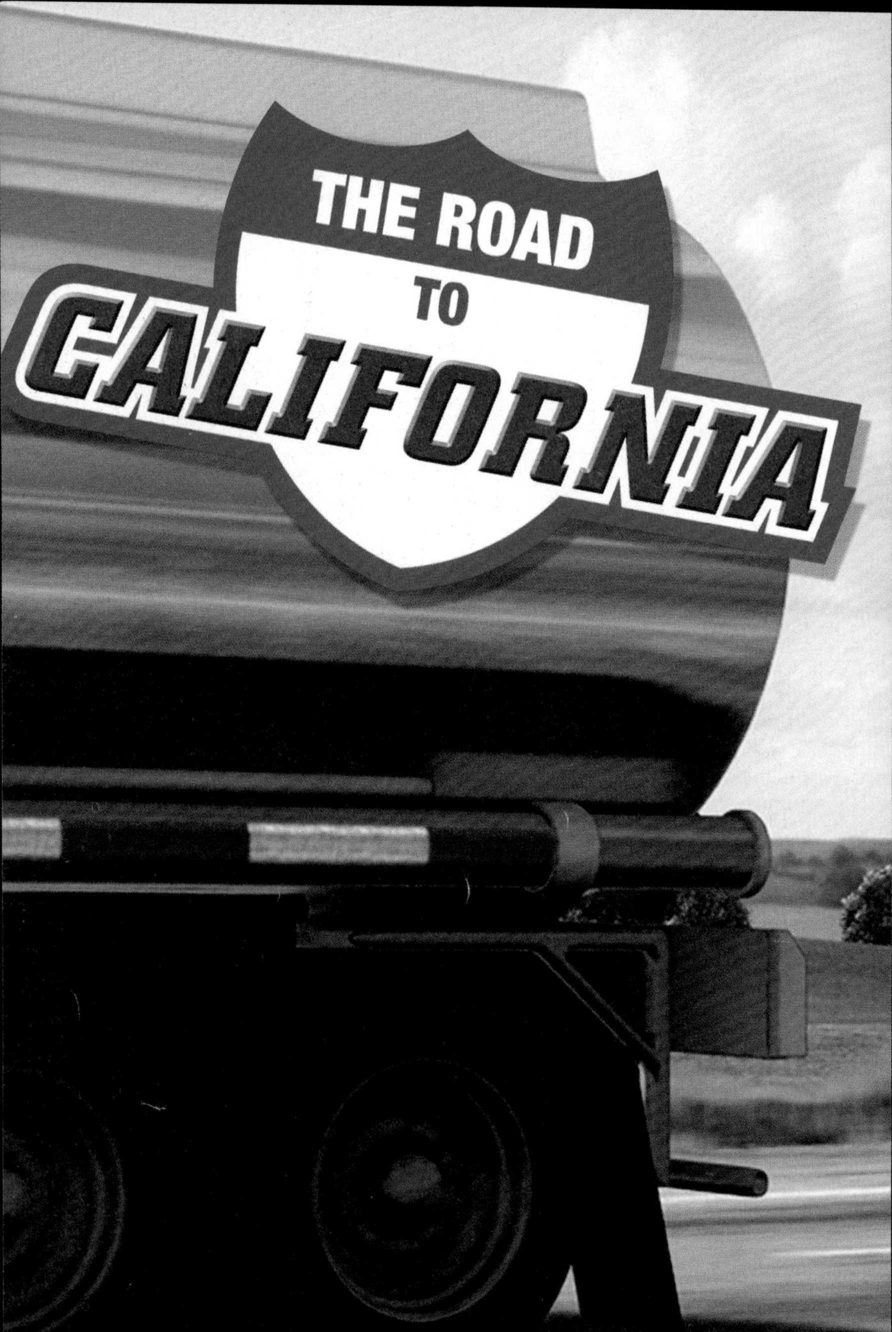
THE ROAD
TO
CALIFORNIA

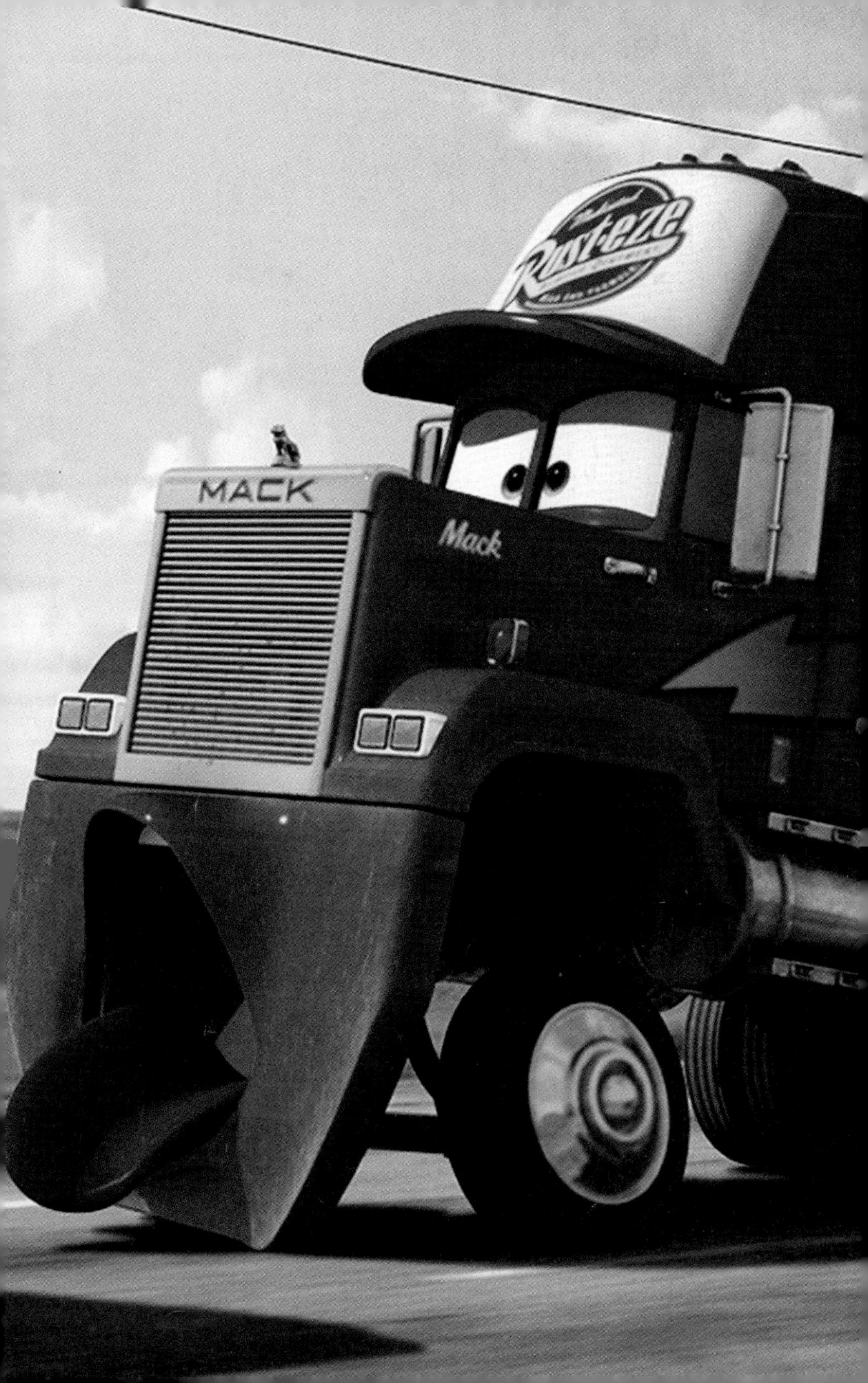
Rust-eze
MACK
Mack

McQueen boards his trailer and his driver Mack starts the journey to California.

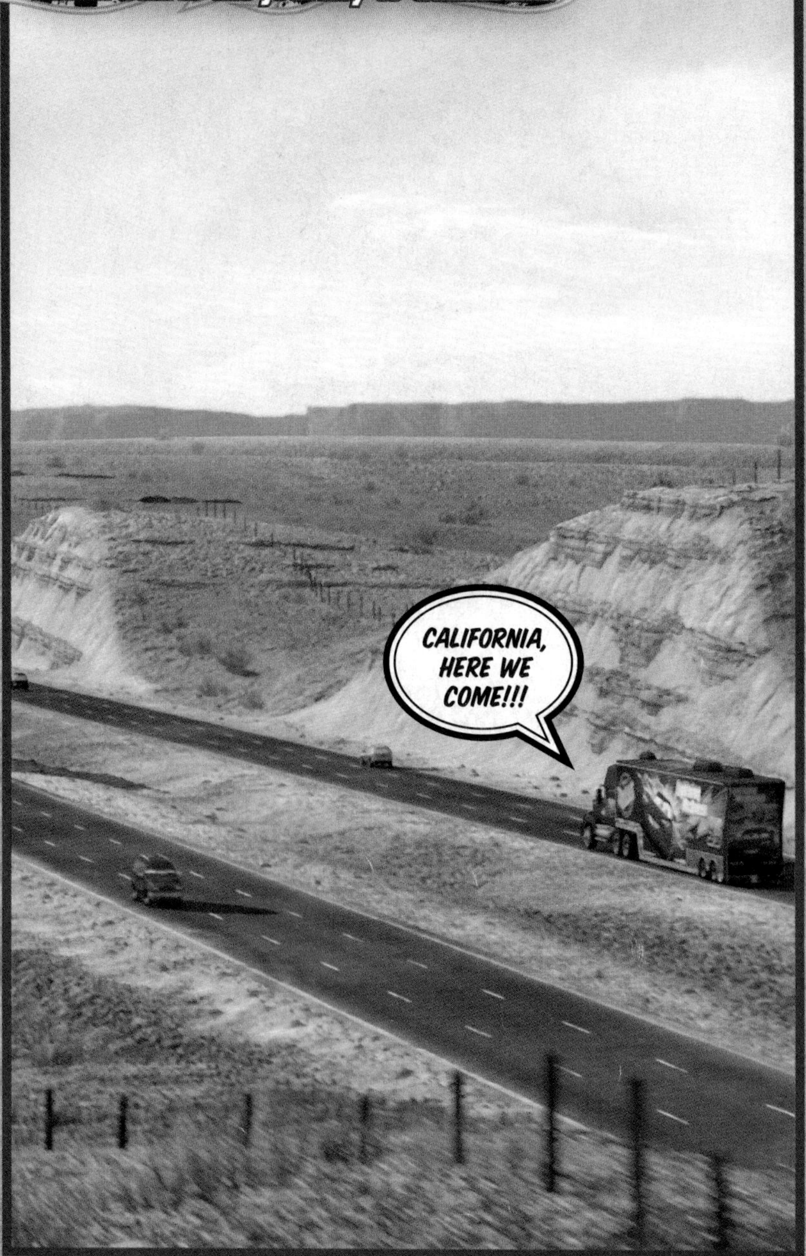
CALIFORNIA, HERE WE COME!!!

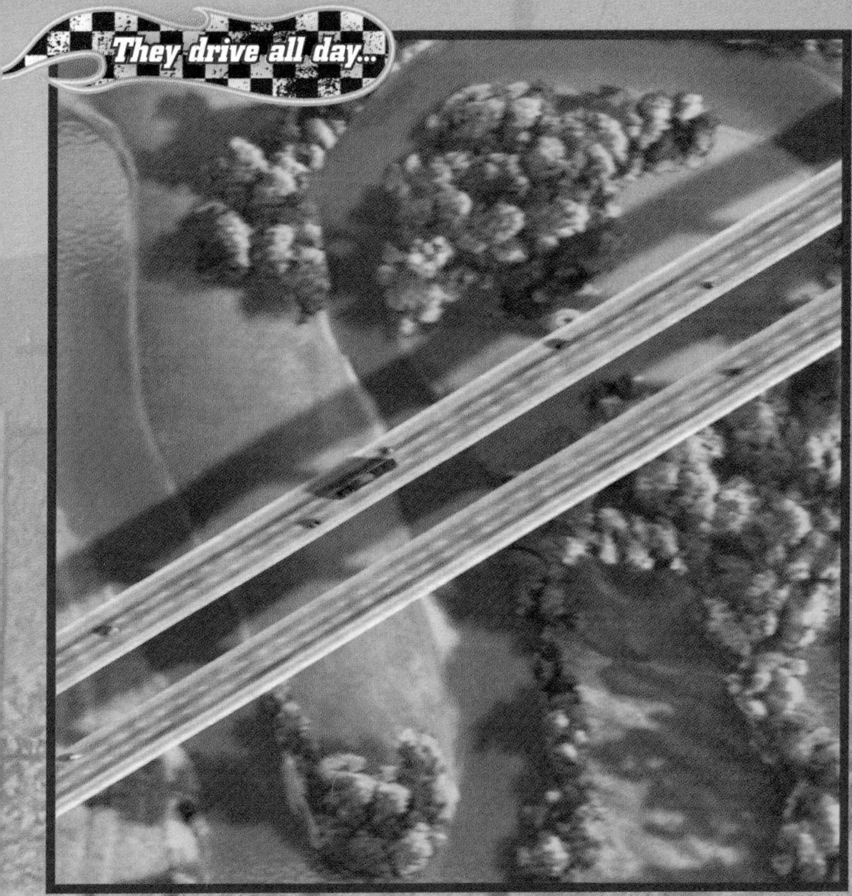

They drive all day...

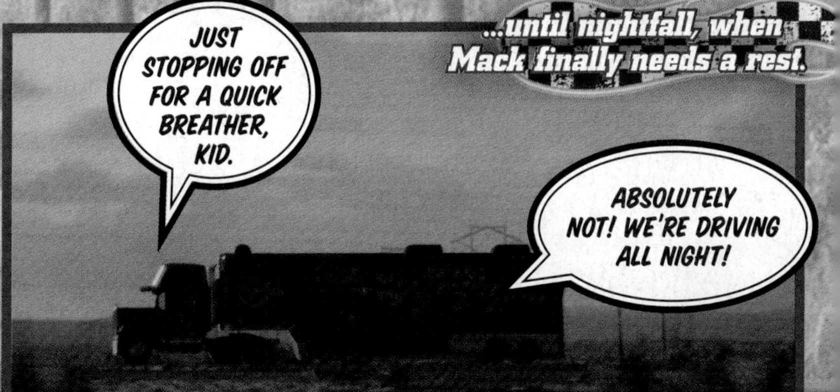

...until nightfall, when Mack finally needs a rest.
JUST STOPPING OFF FOR A QUICK BREATHER, KID.
ABSOLUTELY NOT! WE'RE DRIVING ALL NIGHT!

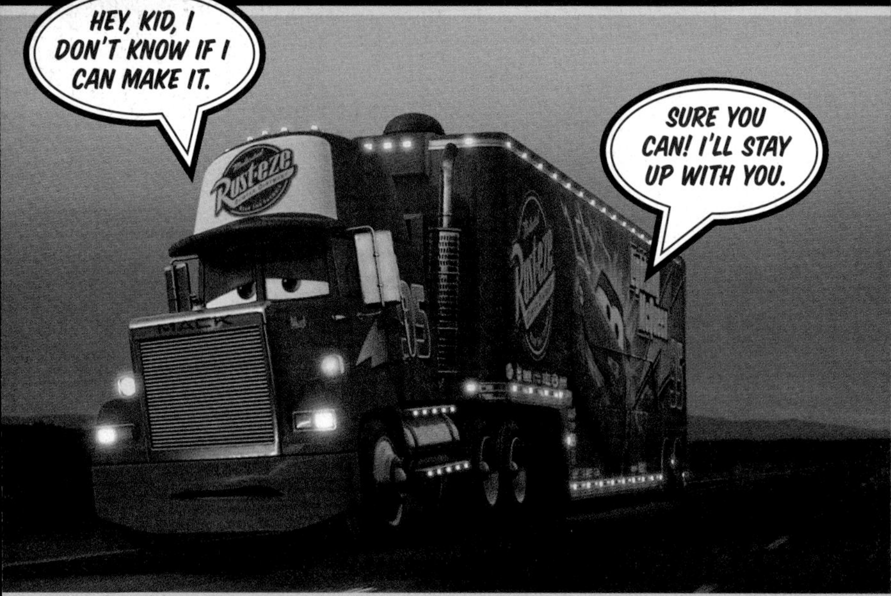
HEY, KID, I DON'T KNOW IF I CAN MAKE IT.
SURE YOU CAN! I'LL STAY UP WITH YOU.

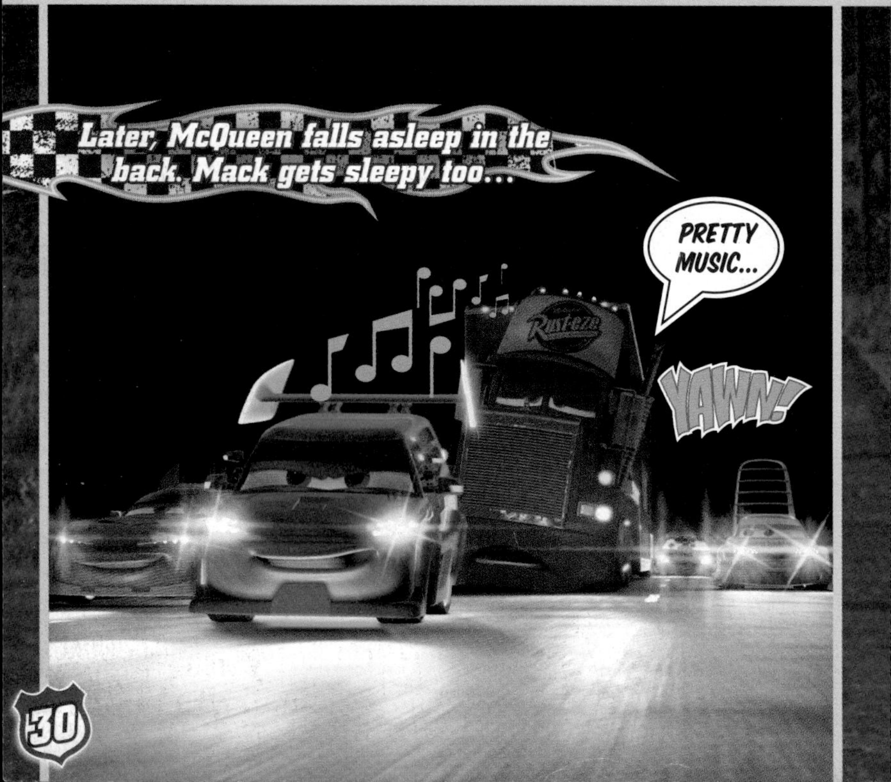
Later, McQueen falls asleep in the back. Mack gets sleepy too...
PRETTY MUSIC...
YAWN!

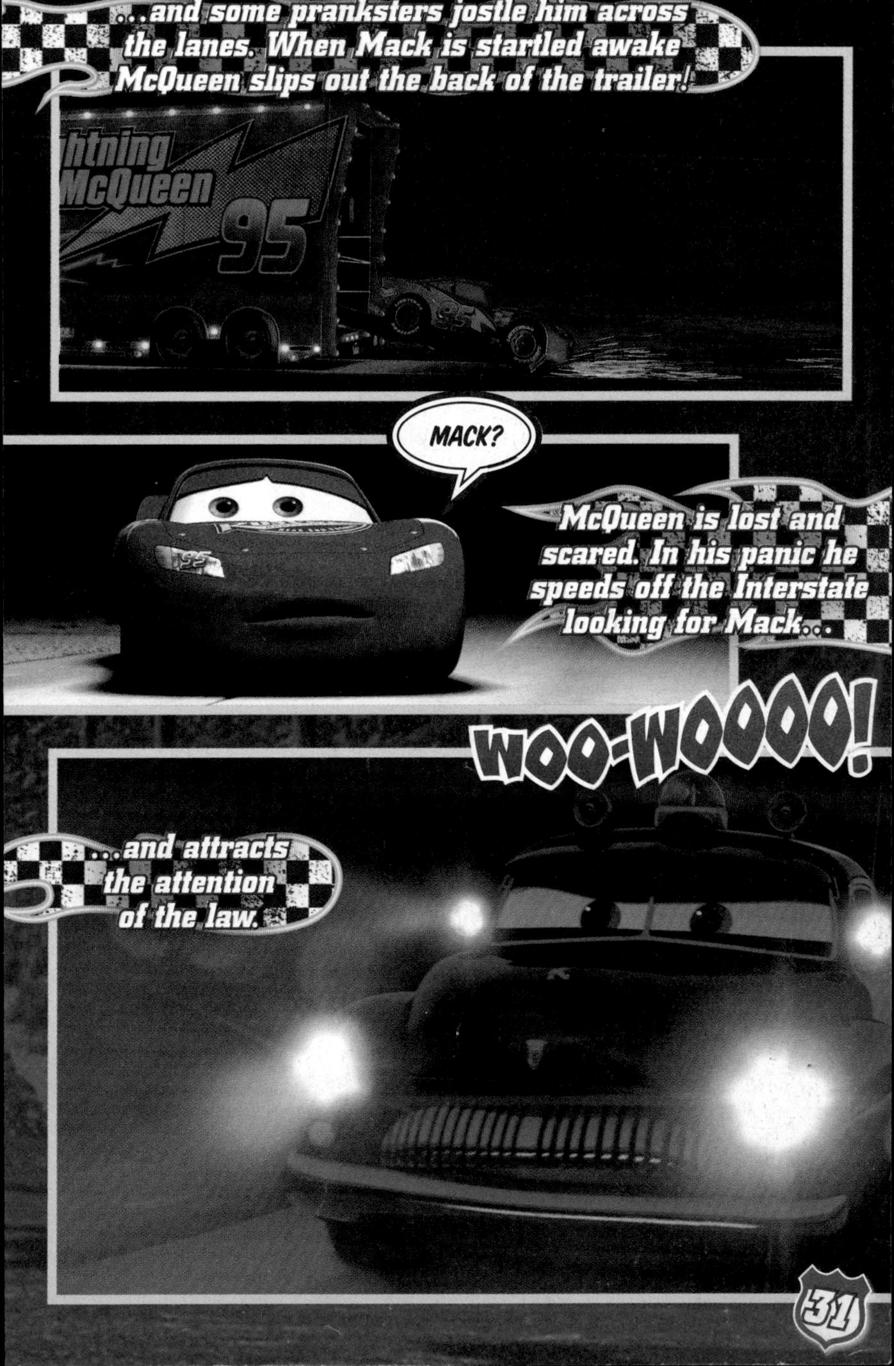
...and some pranksters jostle him across the lanes. When Mack is startled awake McQueen slips out the back of the trailer!
htning McQueen
95
MACK?
McQueen is lost and scared. In his panic he speeds off the Interstate looking for Mack...
WOO-WOOOO!
...and attracts the attention of the law.

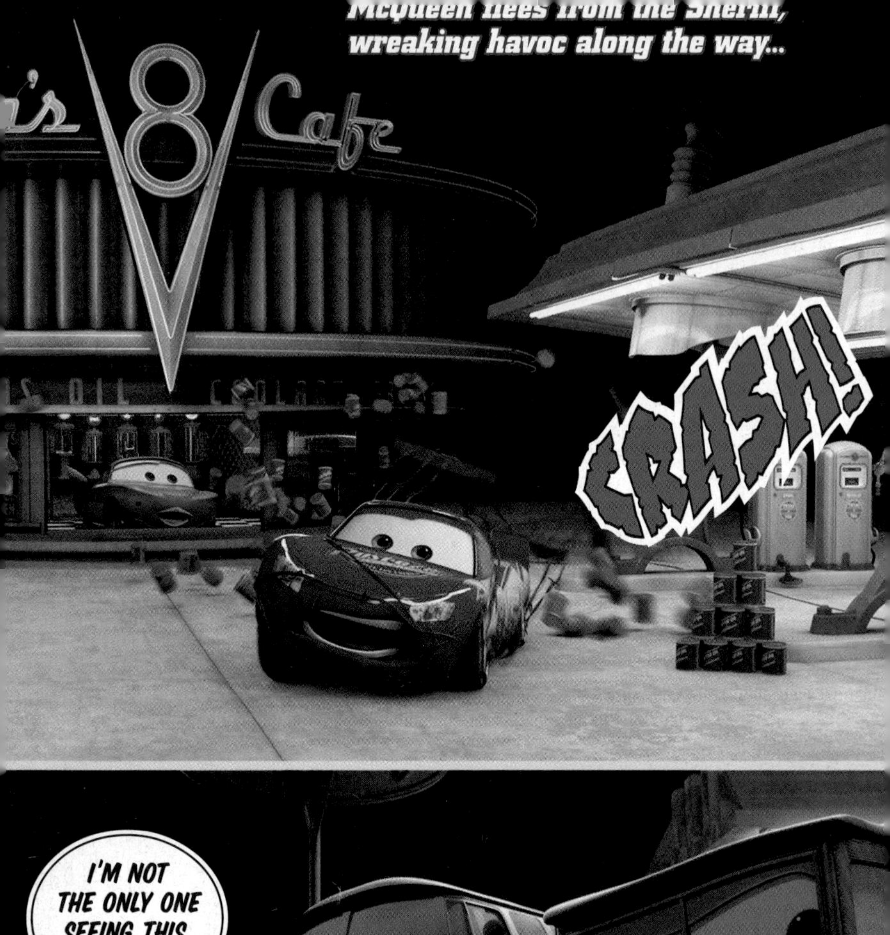
McQueen flees from the Sheriff,
wreaking havoc along the way...
CRASH!

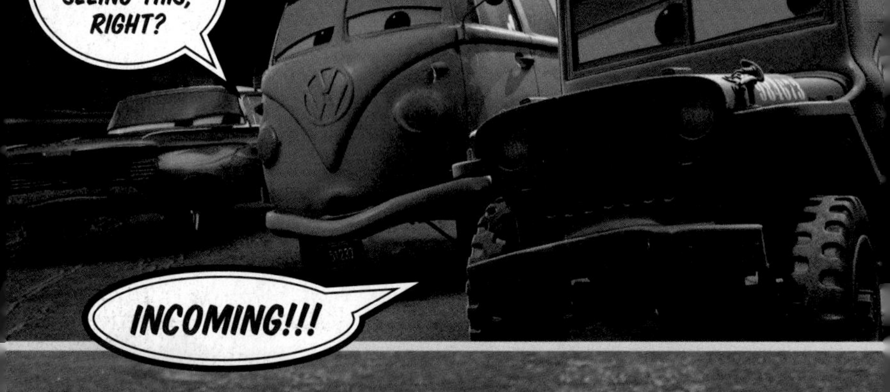
I'M NOT THE ONLY ONE SEEING THIS, RIGHT?
INCOMING!!!

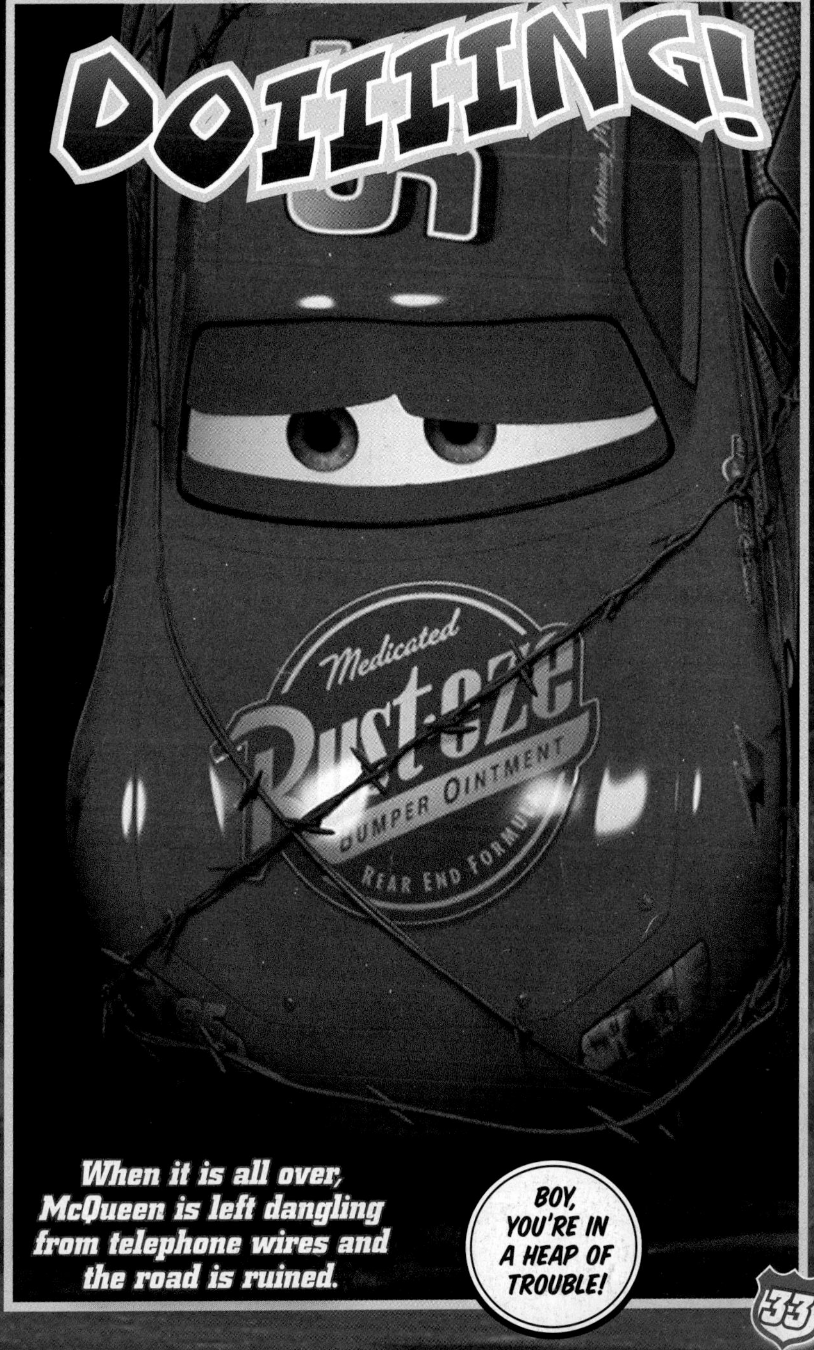
DOIIIING!
Medicated Rust-eze Bumper Ointment Rear End Formula
BOY, YOU'RE IN A HEAP OF TROUBLE!

When it is all over, McQueen is left dangling from telephone wires and the road is ruined.

BREAKING

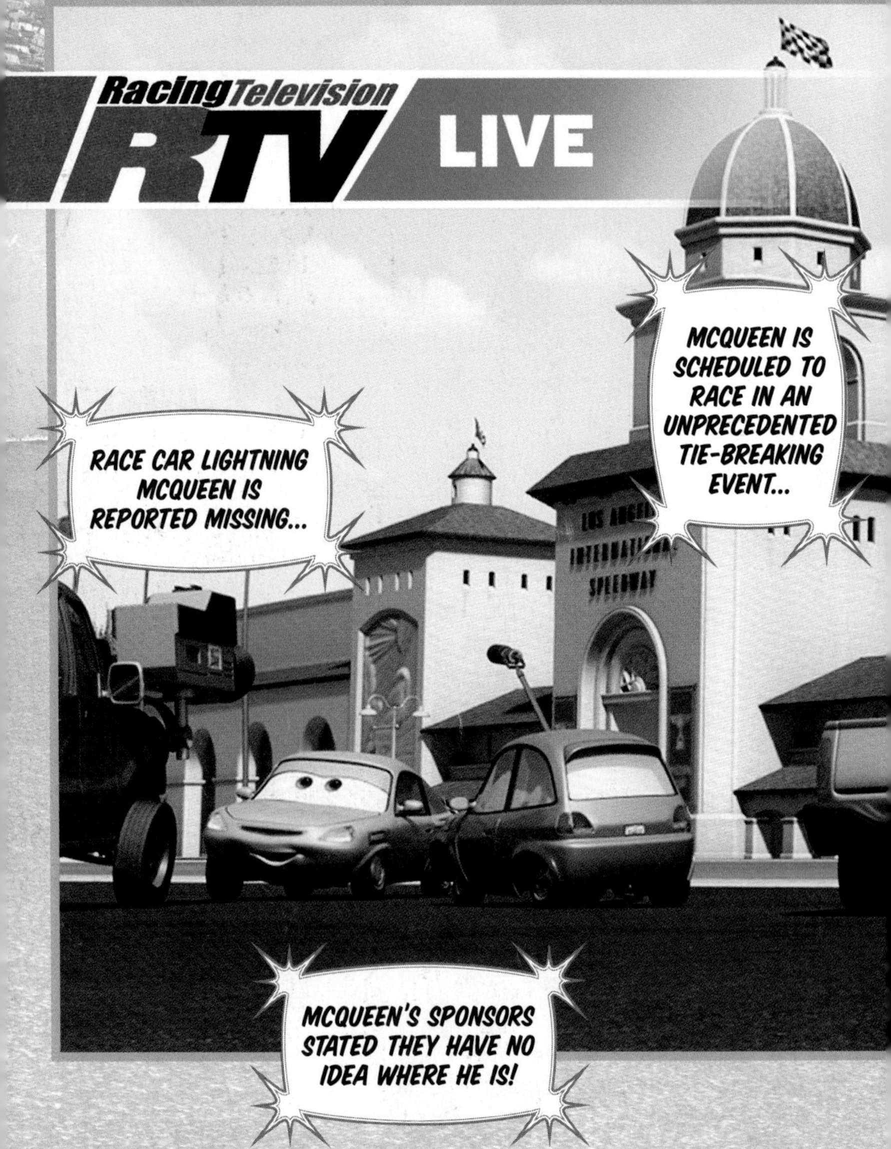
Racing Television
RTV
LIVE
RACE CAR LIGHTNING MCQUEEN IS REPORTED MISSING...
MCQUEEN IS SCHEDULED TO RACE IN AN UNPRECEDENTED TIE-BREAKING EVENT...
MCQUEEN'S SPONSORS STATED THEY HAVE NO IDEA WHERE HE IS!

NEWS

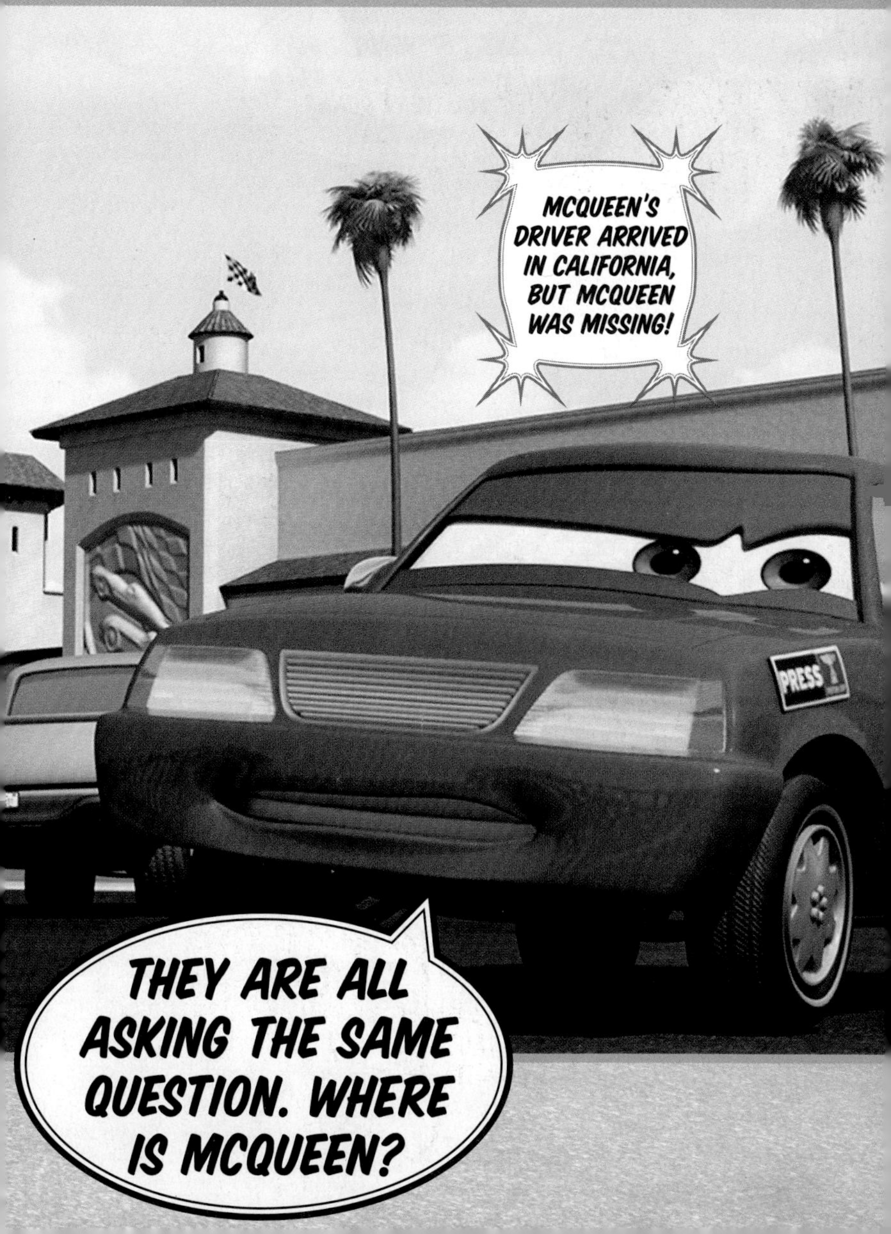
MCQUEEN'S DRIVER ARRIVED IN CALIFORNIA, BUT MCQUEEN WAS MISSING!
PRESS
THEY ARE ALL ASKING THE SAME QUESTION. WHERE IS MCQUEEN?

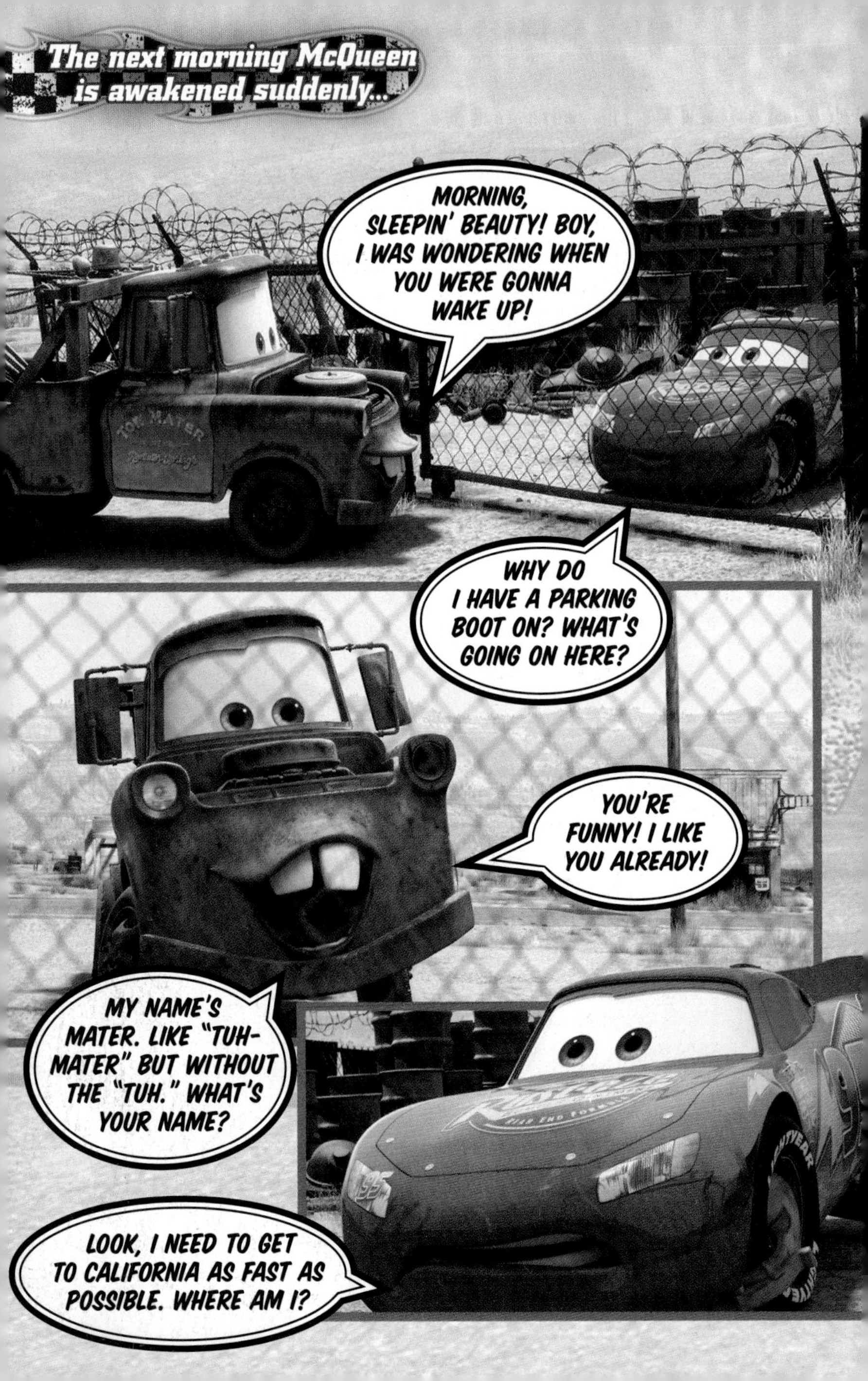
The next morning McQueen is awakened suddenly...
MORNING, SLEEPIN' BEAUTY! BOY, I WAS WONDERING WHEN YOU WERE GONNA WAKE UP!
WHY DO I HAVE A PARKING BOOT ON? WHAT'S GOING ON HERE?
YOU'RE FUNNY! I LIKE YOU ALREADY!
MY NAME'S MATER. LIKE "TUH-MATER" BUT WITHOUT THE "TUH." WHAT'S YOUR NAME?
LOOK, I NEED TO GET TO CALIFORNIA AS FAST AS POSSIBLE. WHERE AM I?

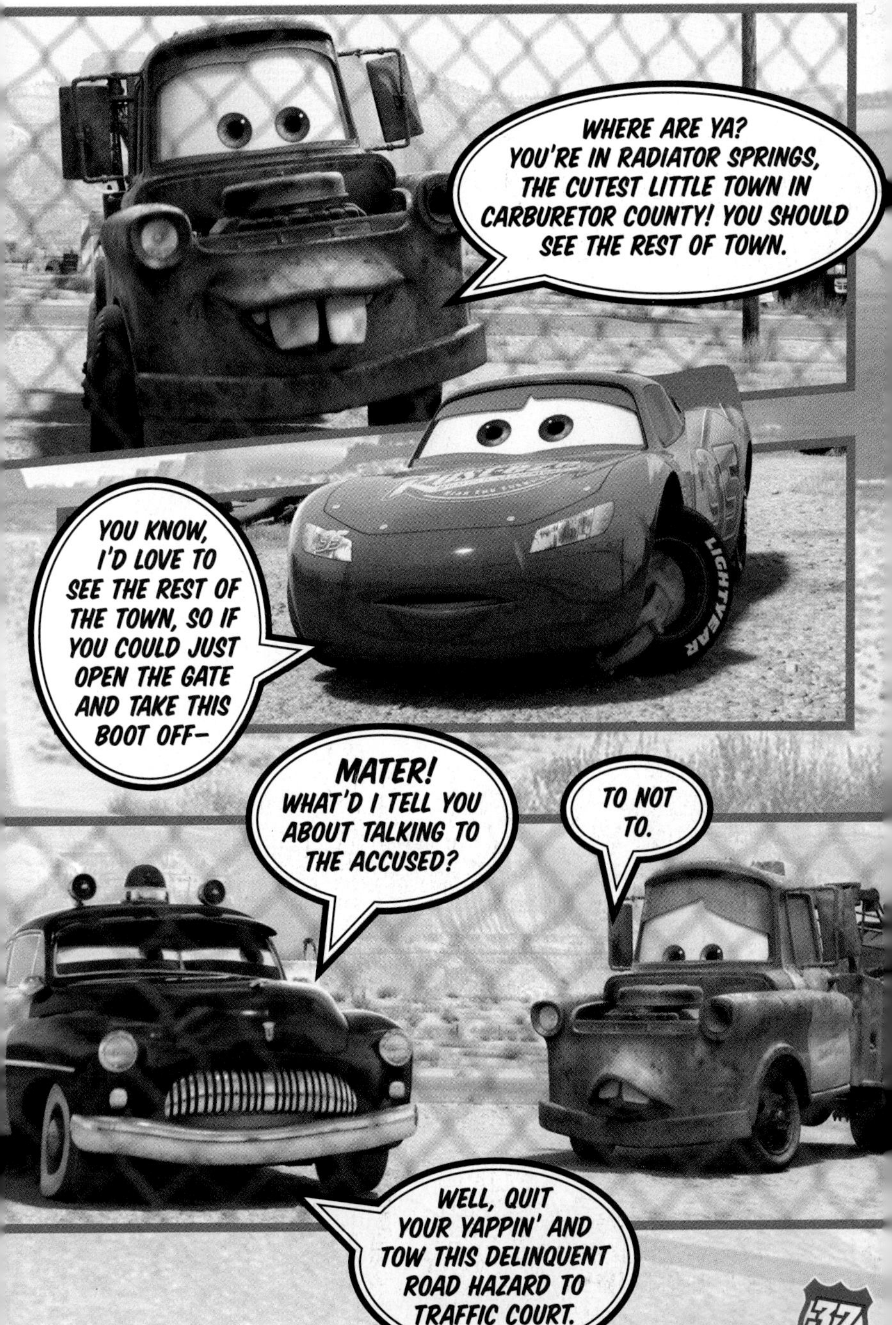
WHERE ARE YA? YOU'RE IN RADIATOR SPRINGS, THE CUTEST LITTLE TOWN IN CARBURETOR COUNTY! YOU SHOULD SEE THE REST OF TOWN.
YOU KNOW, I'D LOVE TO SEE THE REST OF THE TOWN, SO IF YOU COULD JUST OPEN THE GATE AND TAKE THIS BOOT OFF–
LIGHTYEAR
MATER! WHAT'D I TELL YOU ABOUT TALKING TO THE ACCUSED?
TO NOT TO.
WELL, QUIT YOUR YAPPIN' AND TOW THIS DELINQUENT ROAD HAZARD TO TRAFFIC COURT.

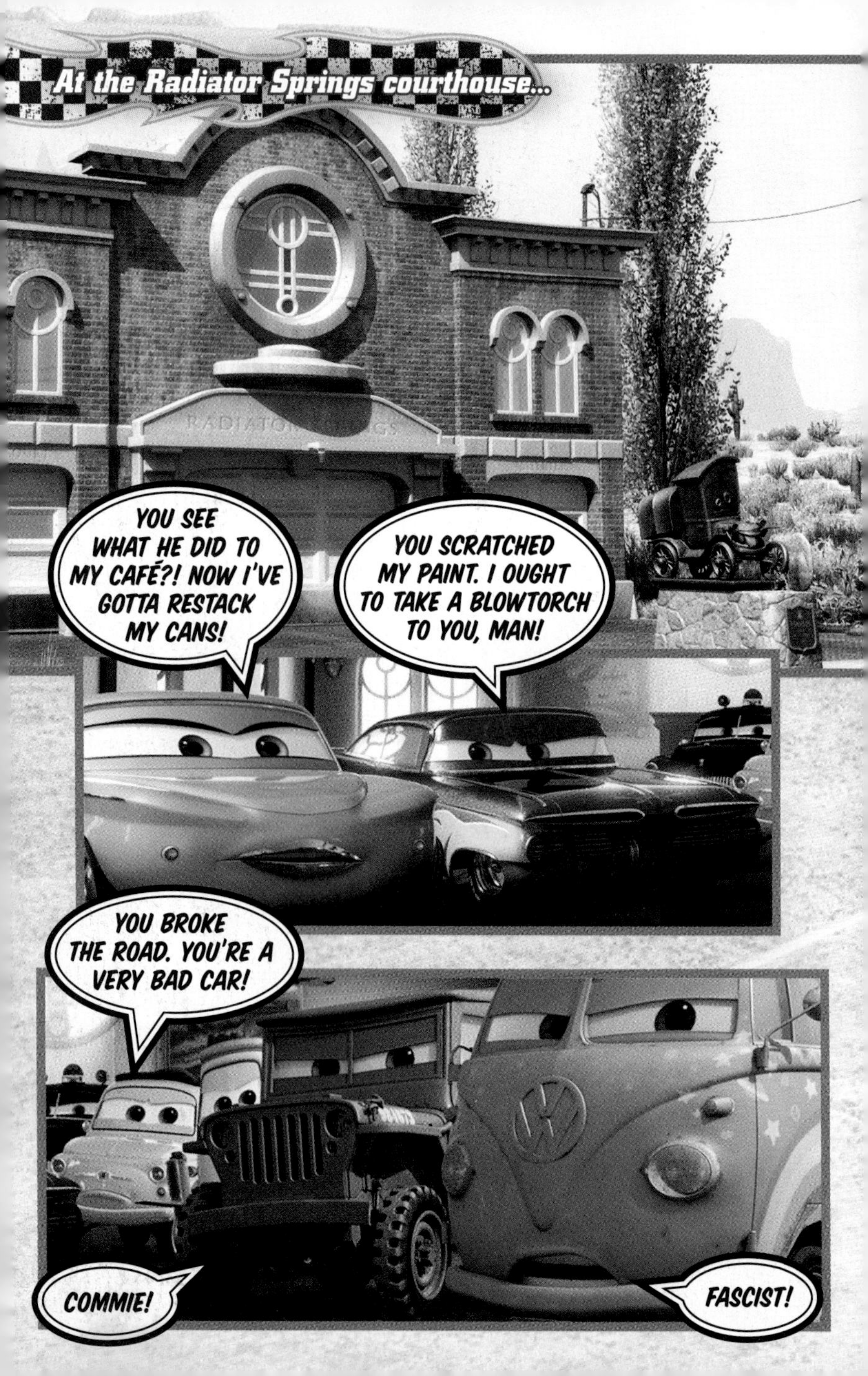
At the Radiator Springs courthouse...
RADIATOR SPRINGS
YOU SEE WHAT HE DID TO MY CAFÉ?! NOW I'VE GOTTA RESTACK MY CANS!
YOU SCRATCHED MY PAINT. I OUGHT TO TAKE A BLOWTORCH TO YOU, MAN!
YOU BROKE THE ROAD. YOU'RE A VERY BAD CAR!
COMMIE!
FASCIST!

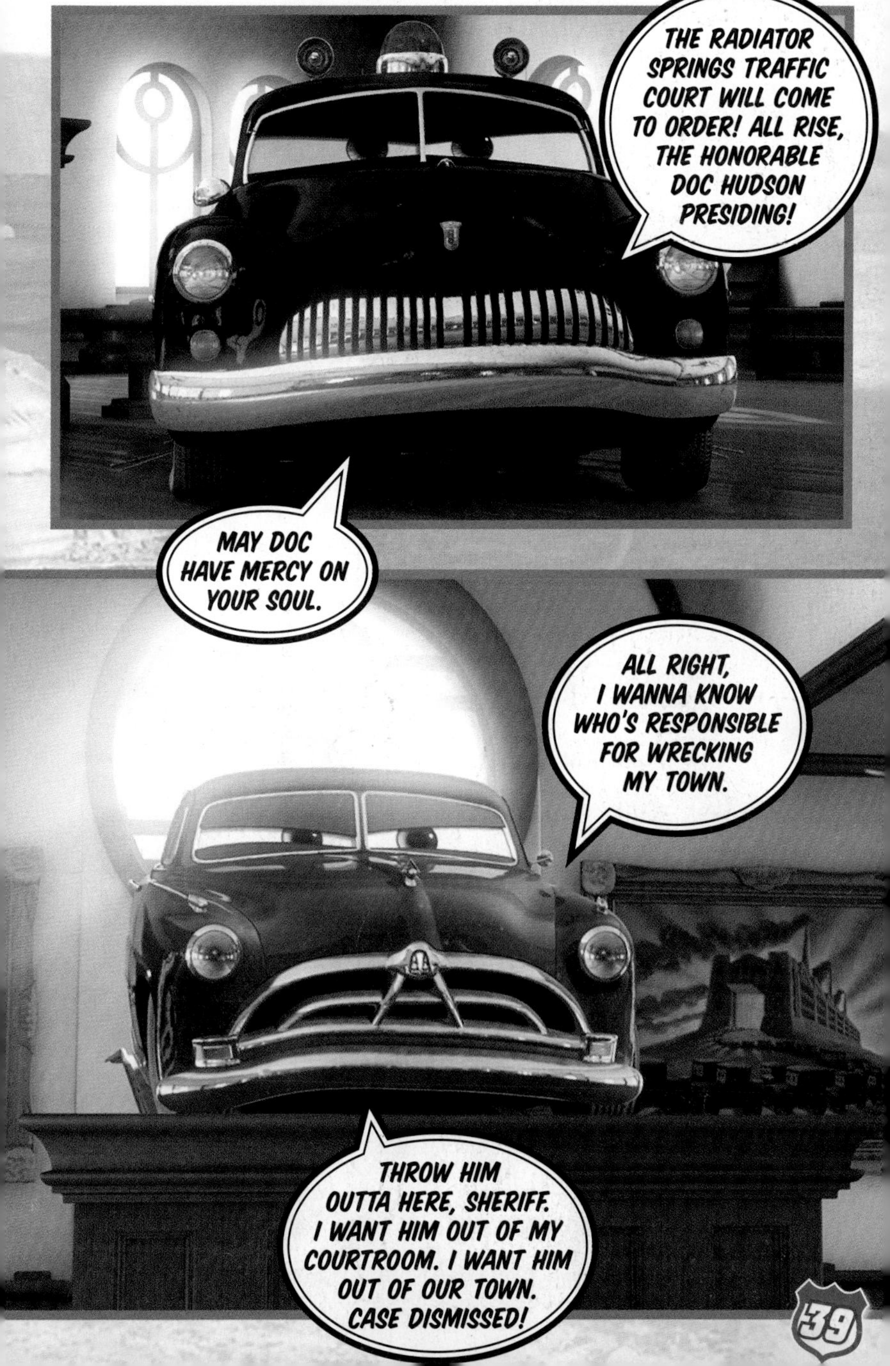
THE RADIATOR SPRINGS TRAFFIC COURT WILL COME TO ORDER! ALL RISE, THE HONORABLE DOC HUDSON PRESIDING!
MAY DOC HAVE MERCY ON YOUR SOUL.
ALL RIGHT, I WANNA KNOW WHO'S RESPONSIBLE FOR WRECKING MY TOWN.
THROW HIM OUTTA HERE, SHERIFF. I WANT HIM OUT OF MY COURTROOM. I WANT HIM OUT OF OUR TOWN. CASE DISMISSED!

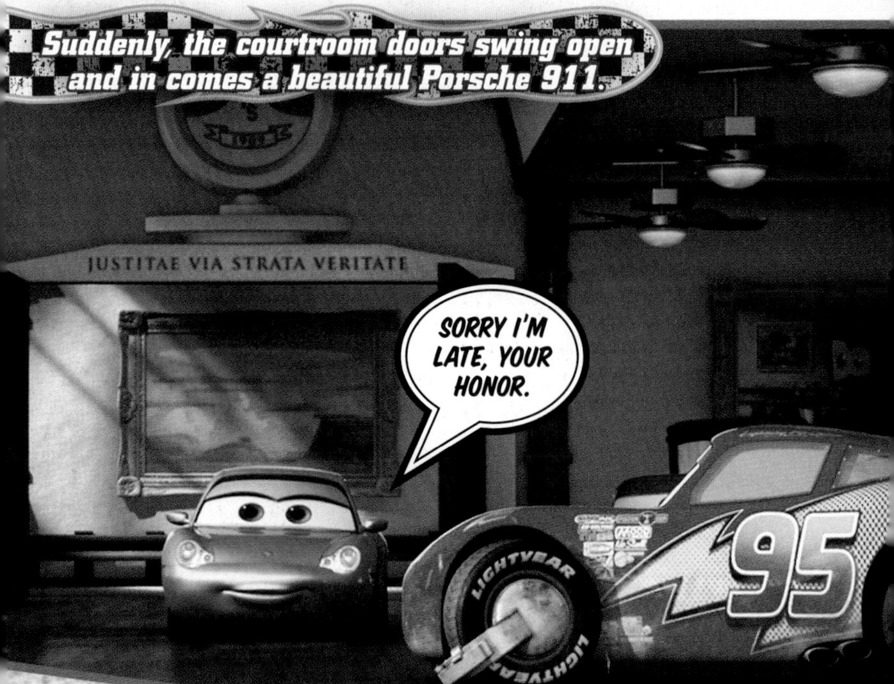
Suddenly, the courtroom doors swing open and in comes a beautiful Porsche 911.
JUSTITAE VIA STRATA VERITATE
SORRY I'M LATE, YOUR HONOR.
LIGHTYEAR
95

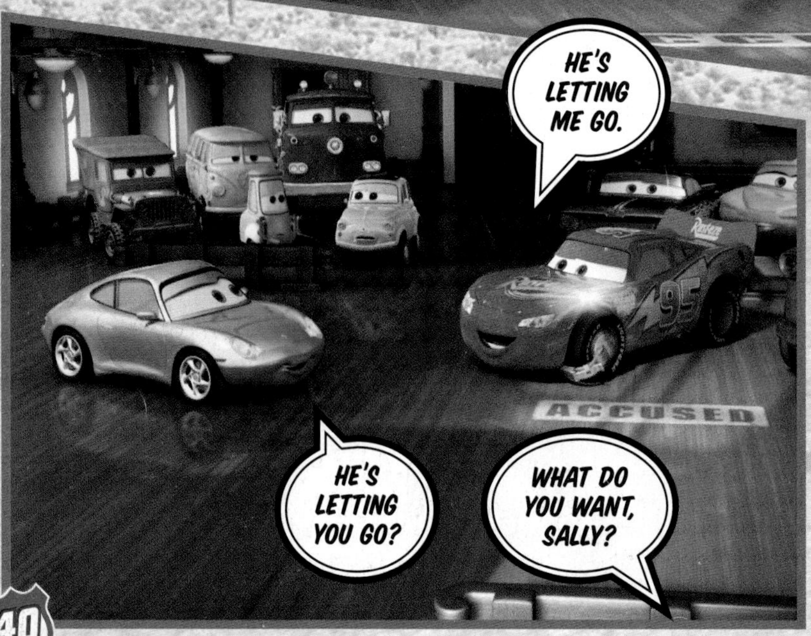
HE'S LETTING ME GO.
ACCUSED
HE'S LETTING YOU GO?
WHAT DO YOU WANT, SALLY?

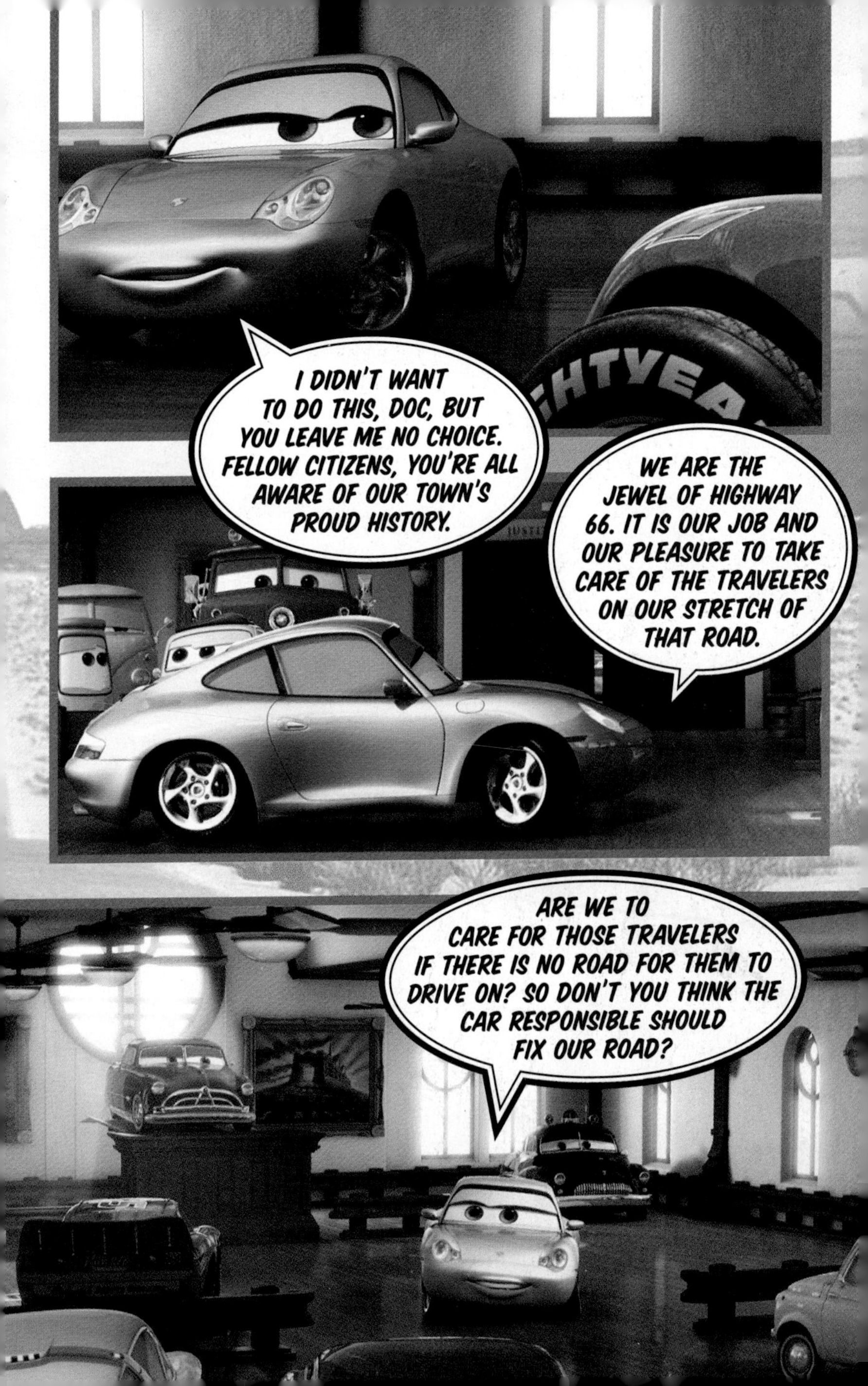
I DIDN'T WANT TO DO THIS, DOC, BUT YOU LEAVE ME NO CHOICE. FELLOW CITIZENS, YOU'RE ALL AWARE OF OUR TOWN'S PROUD HISTORY.
WE ARE THE JEWEL OF HIGHWAY 66. IT IS OUR JOB AND OUR PLEASURE TO TAKE CARE OF THE TRAVELERS ON OUR STRETCH OF THAT ROAD.
ARE WE TO CARE FOR THOSE TRAVELERS IF THERE IS NO ROAD FOR THEM TO DRIVE ON? SO DON'T YOU THINK THE CAR RESPONSIBLE SHOULD FIX OUR ROAD?

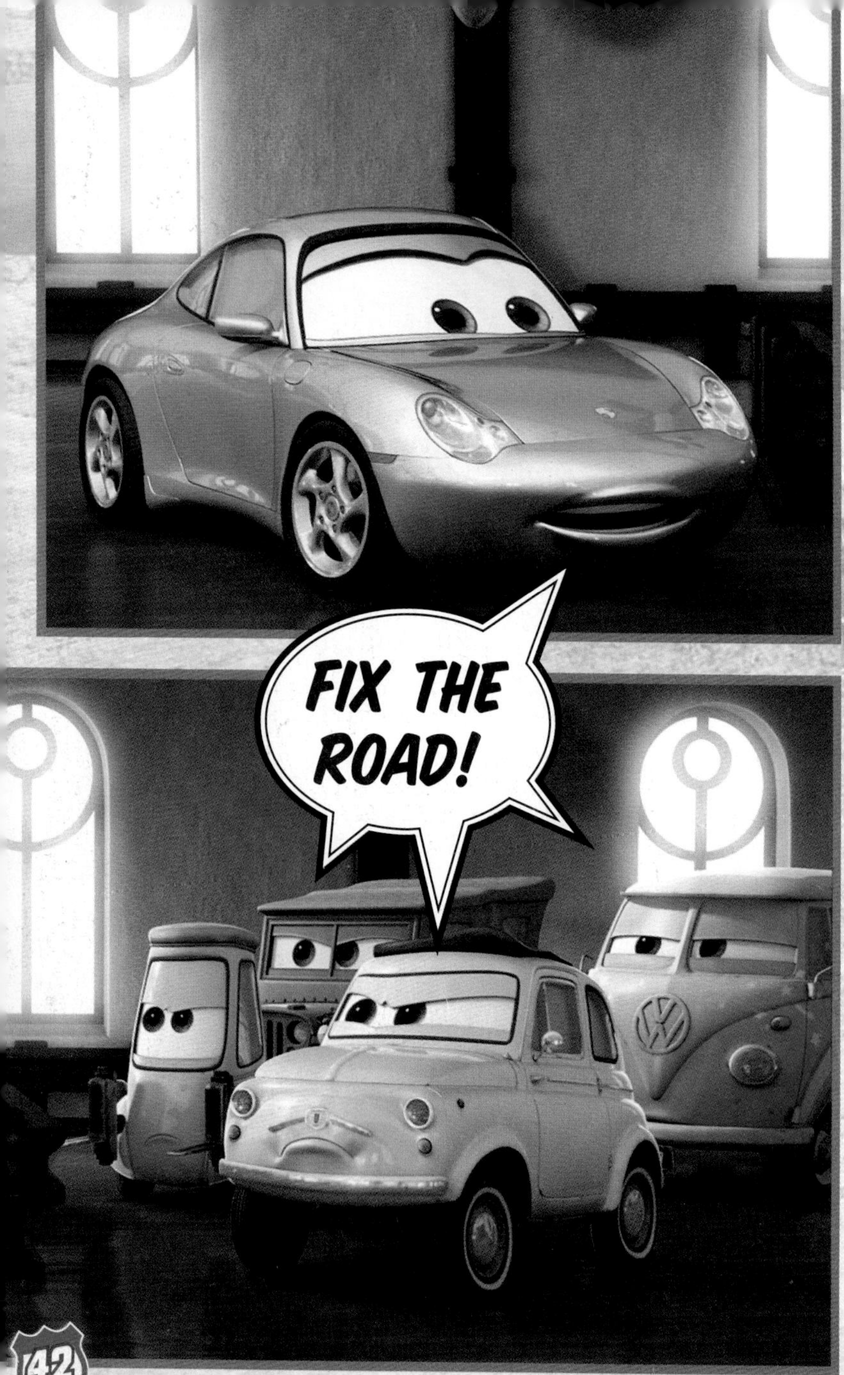
FIX THE ROAD!

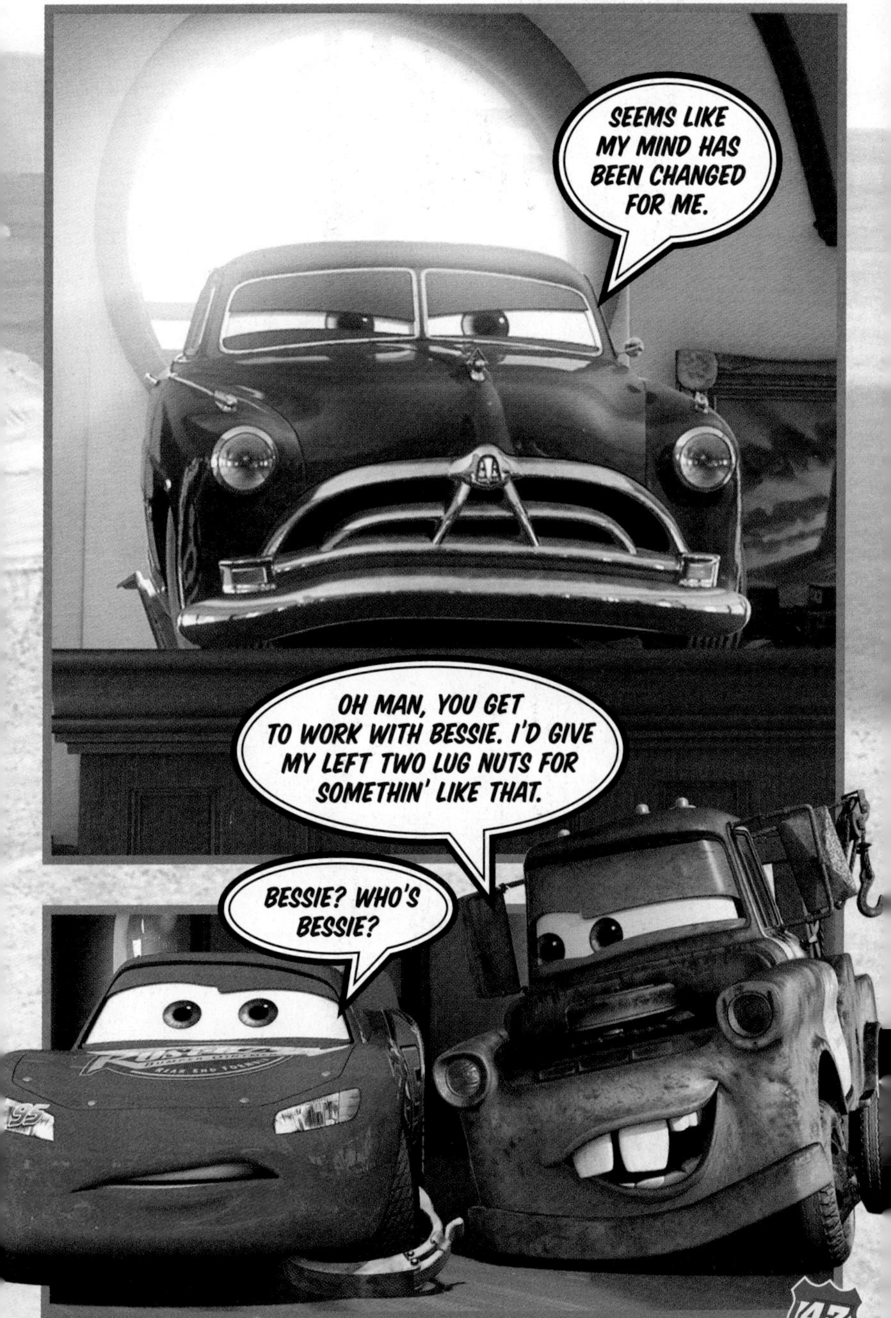
SEEMS LIKE MY MIND HAS BEEN CHANGED FOR ME.
OH MAN, YOU GET TO WORK WITH BESSIE. I'D GIVE MY LEFT TWO LUG NUTS FOR SOMETHIN' LIKE THAT.
BESSIE? WHO'S BESSIE?

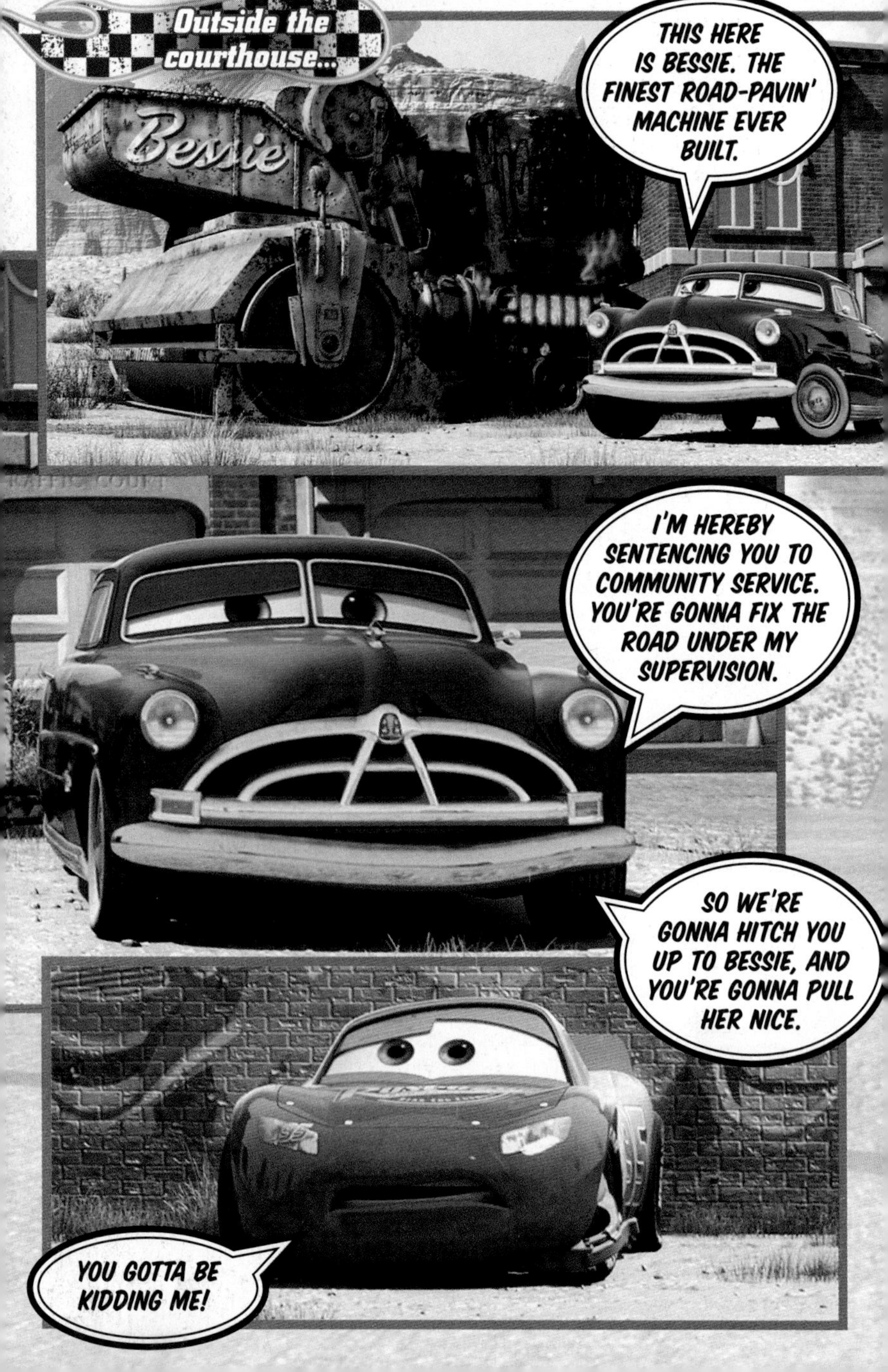
Outside the courthouse...
THIS HERE IS BESSIE. THE FINEST ROAD-PAVIN' MACHINE EVER BUILT.
Bessie
I'M HEREBY SENTENCING YOU TO COMMUNITY SERVICE. YOU'RE GONNA FIX THE ROAD UNDER MY SUPERVISION.
SO WE'RE GONNA HITCH YOU UP TO BESSIE, AND YOU'RE GONNA PULL HER NICE.
YOU GOTTA BE KIDDING ME!

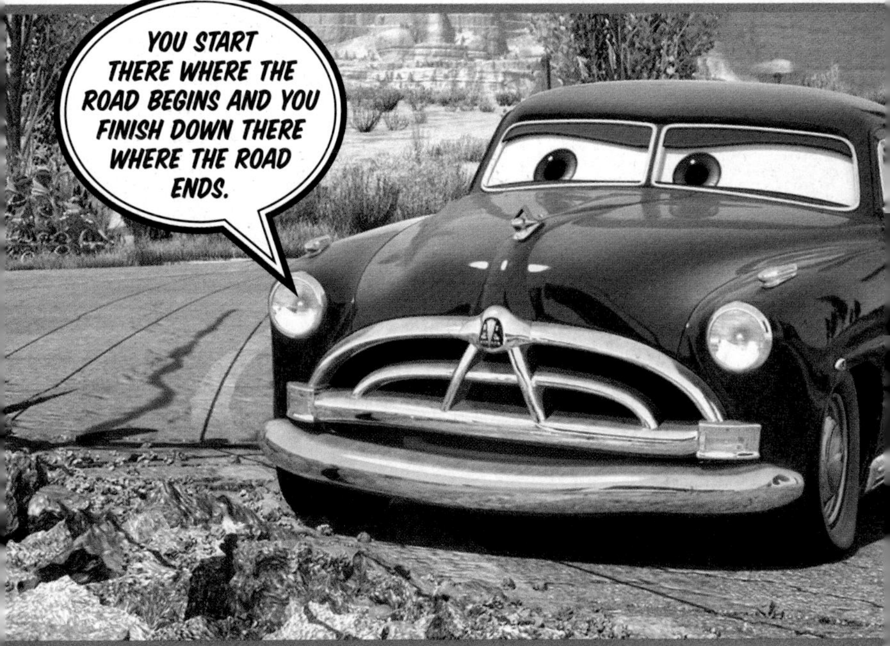
YOU START THERE WHERE THE ROAD BEGINS AND YOU FINISH DOWN THERE WHERE THE ROAD ENDS.

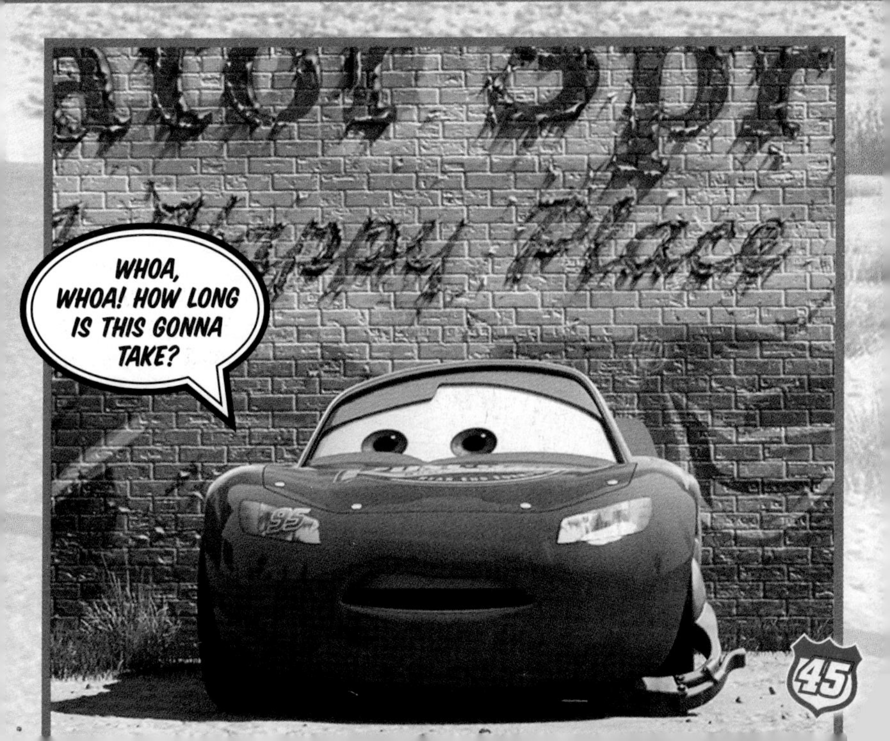
WHOA, WHOA! HOW LONG IS THIS GONNA TAKE?

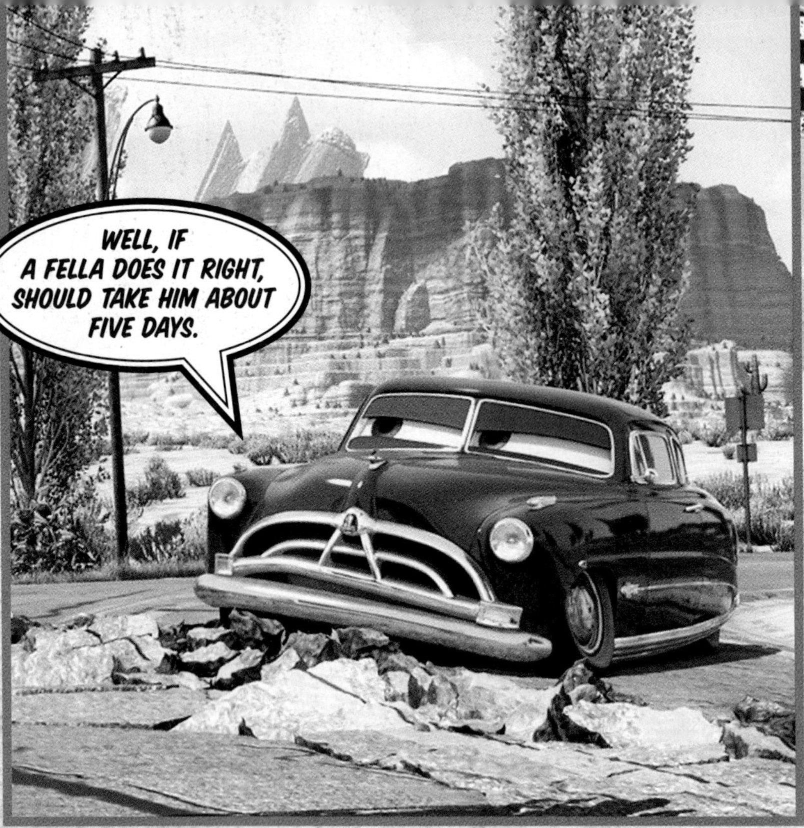
WELL, IF A FELLA DOES IT RIGHT, SHOULD TAKE HIM ABOUT FIVE DAYS.

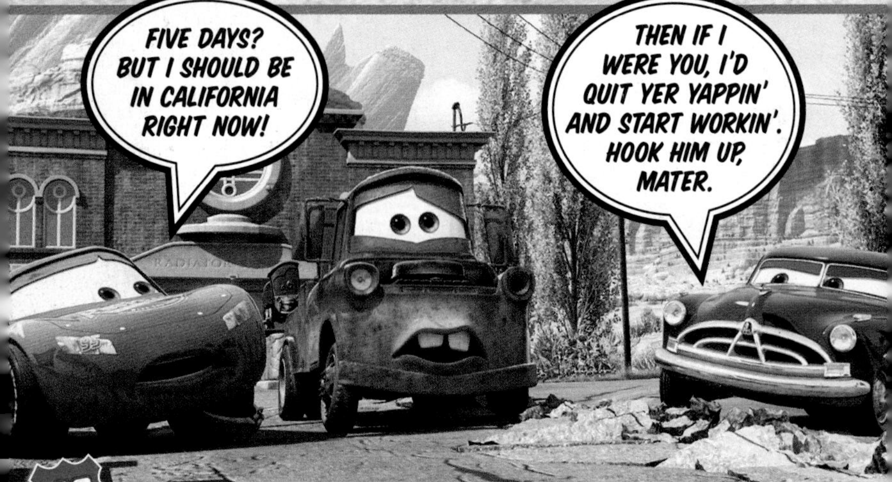
FIVE DAYS? BUT I SHOULD BE IN CALIFORNIA RIGHT NOW!
THEN IF I WERE YOU, I'D QUIT YER YAPPIN' AND START WORKIN'. HOOK HIM UP, MATER.

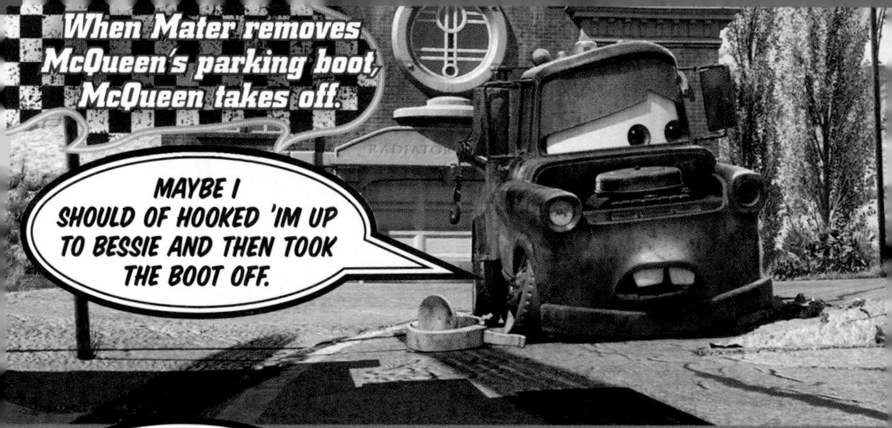
When Mater removes McQueen's parking boot, McQueen takes off.
MAYBE I SHOULD OF HOOKED 'IM UP TO BESSIE AND THEN TOOK THE BOOT OFF.

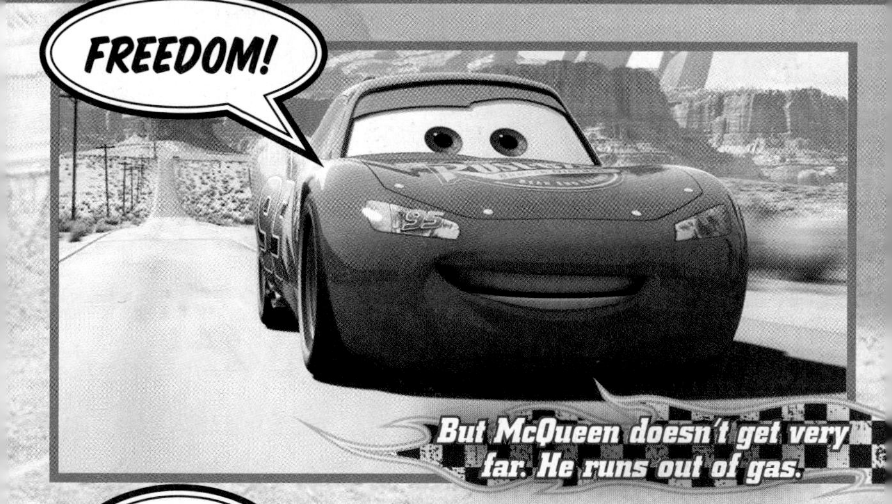
FREEDOM!
But McQueen doesn't get very far. He runs out of gas.

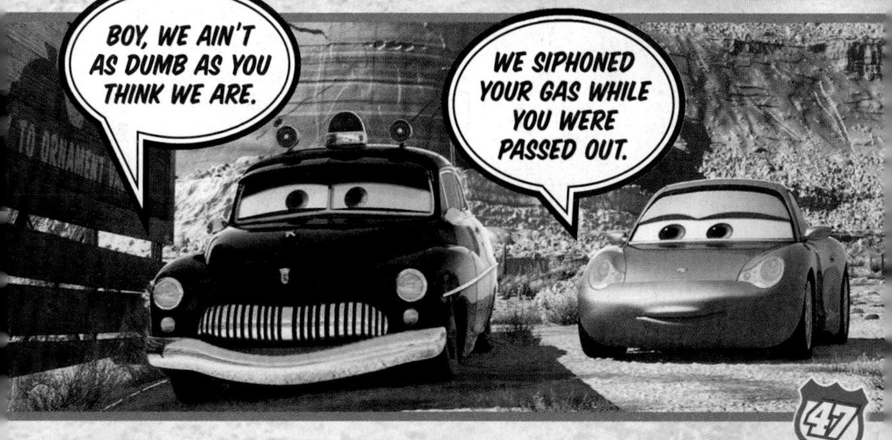
BOY, WE AIN'T AS DUMB AS YOU THINK WE ARE.
WE SIPHONED YOUR GAS WHILE YOU WERE PASSED OUT.

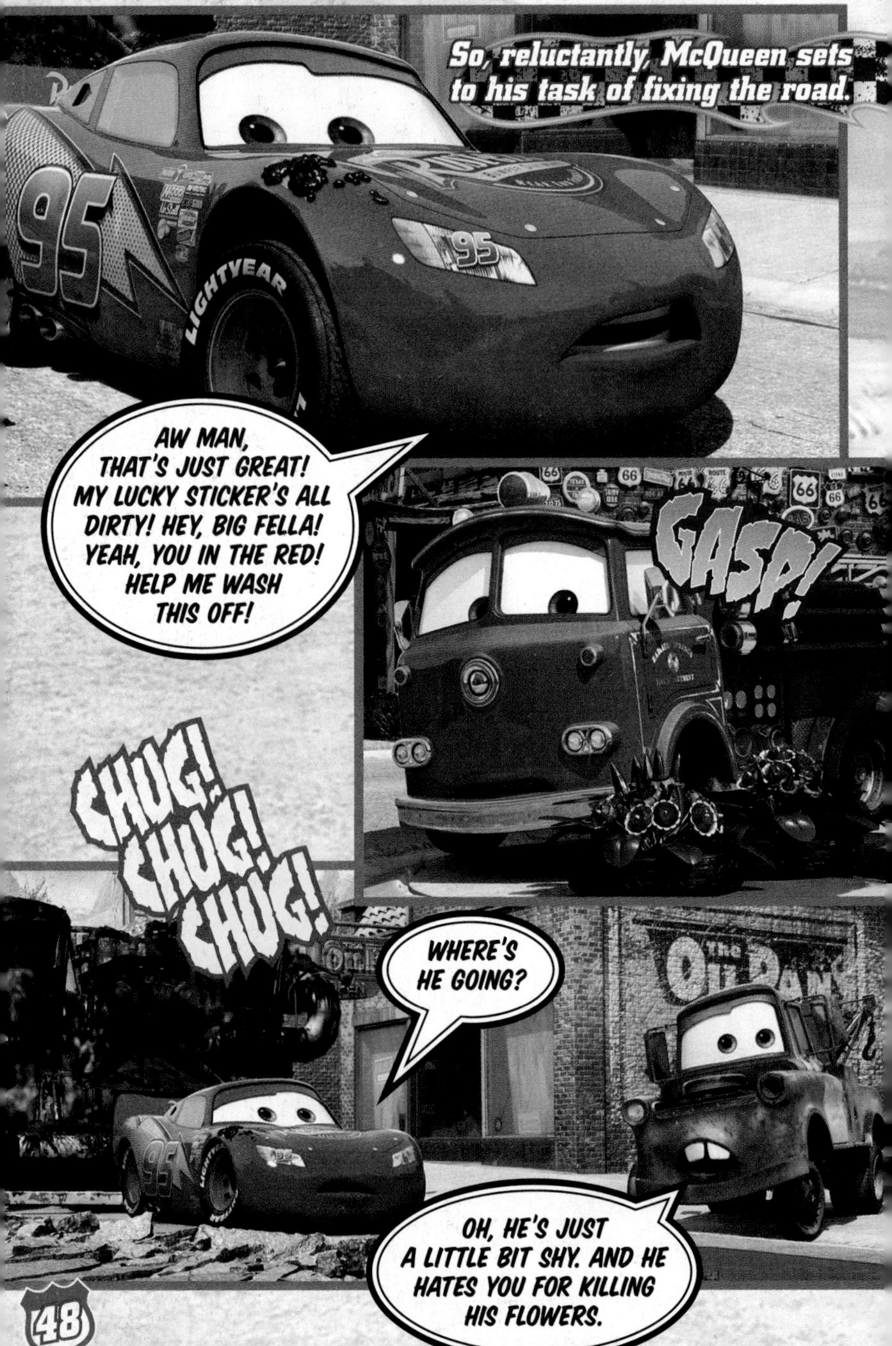
So, reluctantly, McQueen sets to his task of fixing the road.
AW MAN, THAT'S JUST GREAT! MY LUCKY STICKER'S ALL DIRTY! HEY, BIG FELLA! YEAH, YOU IN THE RED! HELP ME WASH THIS OFF!
GASP!
CHUG! CHUG! CHUG!
WHERE'S HE GOING?
OH, HE'S JUST A LITTLE BIT SHY. AND HE HATES YOU FOR KILLING HIS FLOWERS.

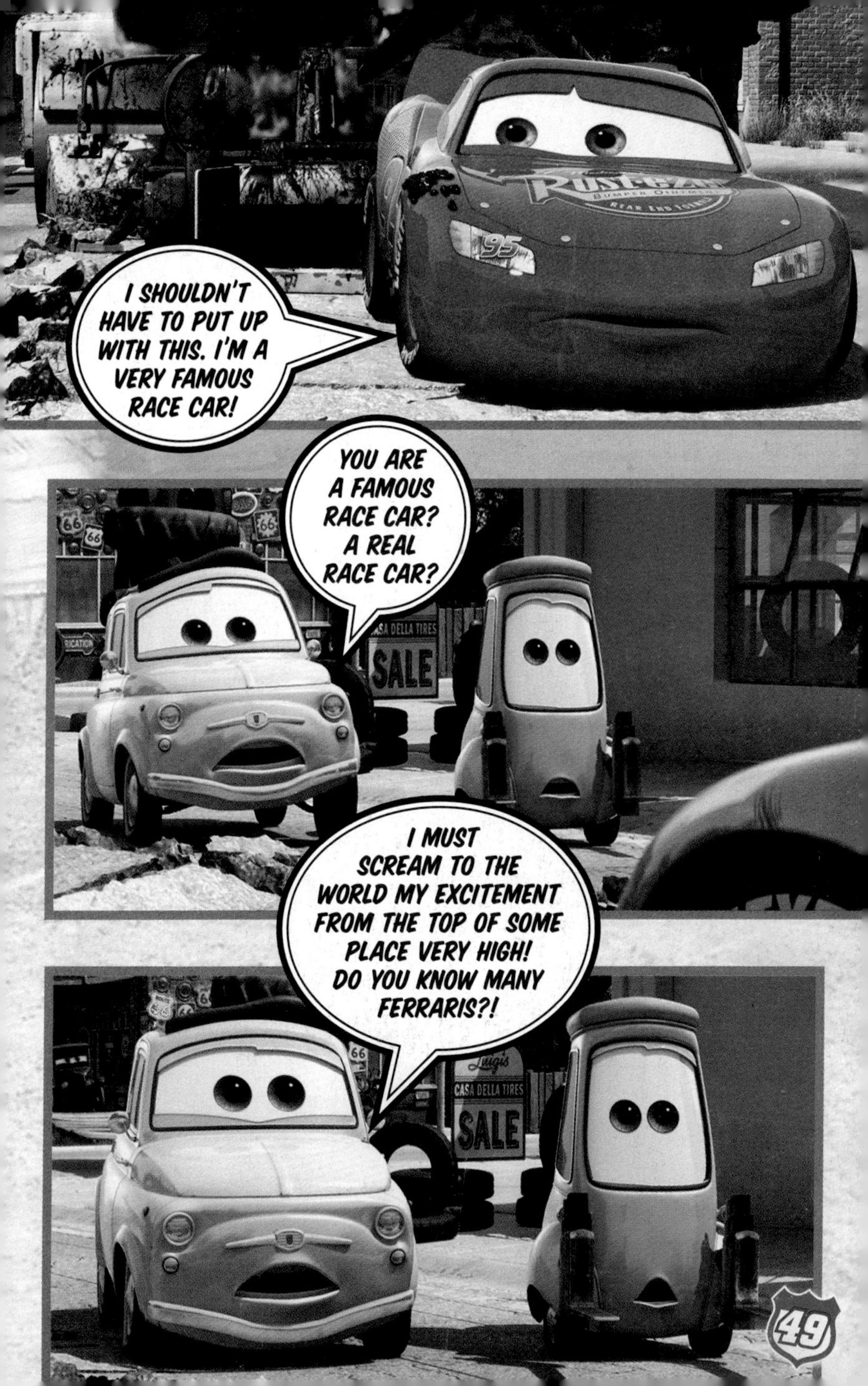
I SHOULDN'T HAVE TO PUT UP WITH THIS. I'M A VERY FAMOUS RACE CAR!
YOU ARE A FAMOUS RACE CAR? A REAL RACE CAR?
I MUST SCREAM TO THE WORLD MY EXCITEMENT FROM THE TOP OF SOME PLACE VERY HIGH! DO YOU KNOW MANY FERRARIS?!

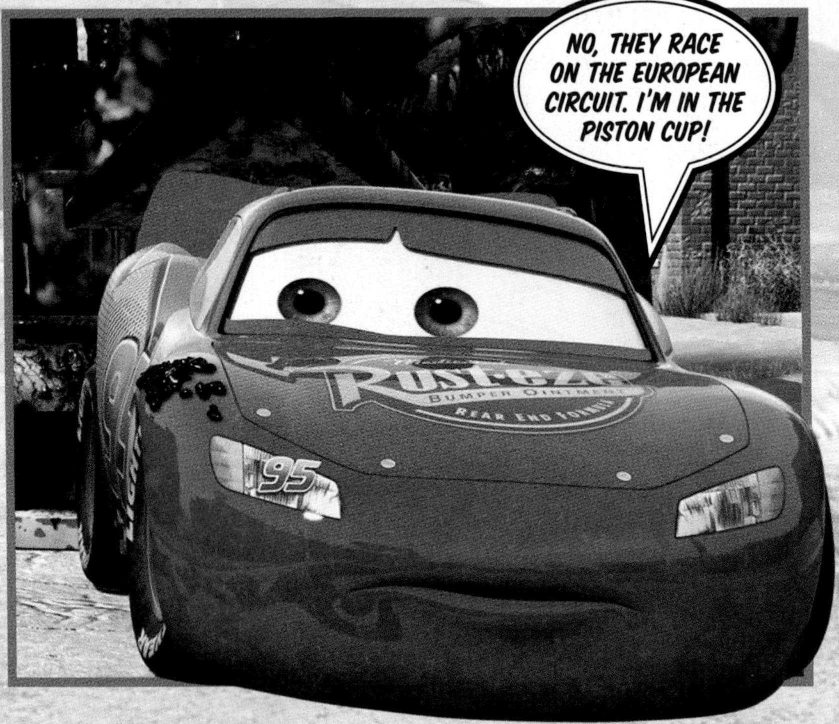
NO, THEY RACE ON THE EUROPEAN CIRCUIT. I'M IN THE PISTON CUP!
Rust-eze
BUMPER OINTMENT
REAR END FORMULA
95

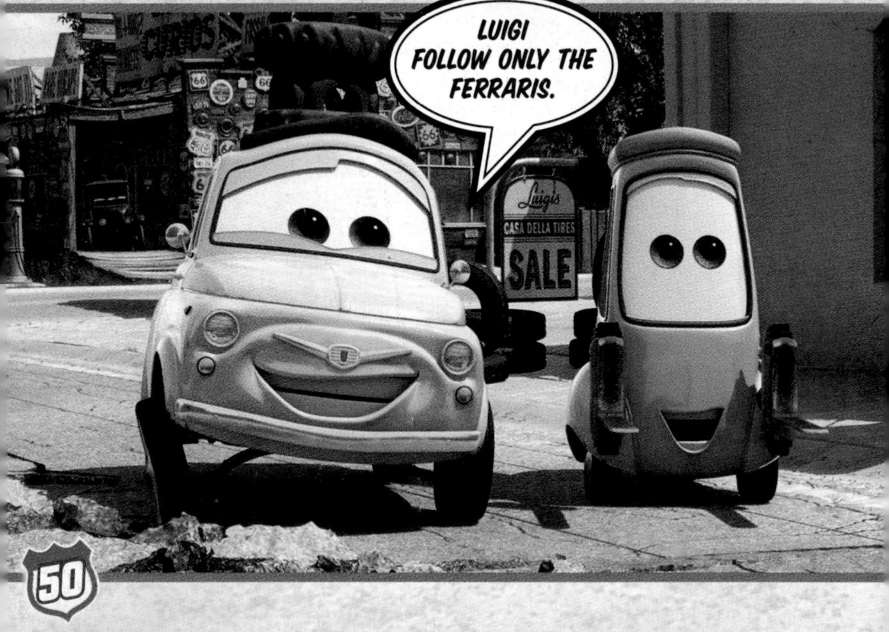
LUIGI FOLLOW ONLY THE FERRARIS.
Luigi's
CASA DELLA TIRES
SALE

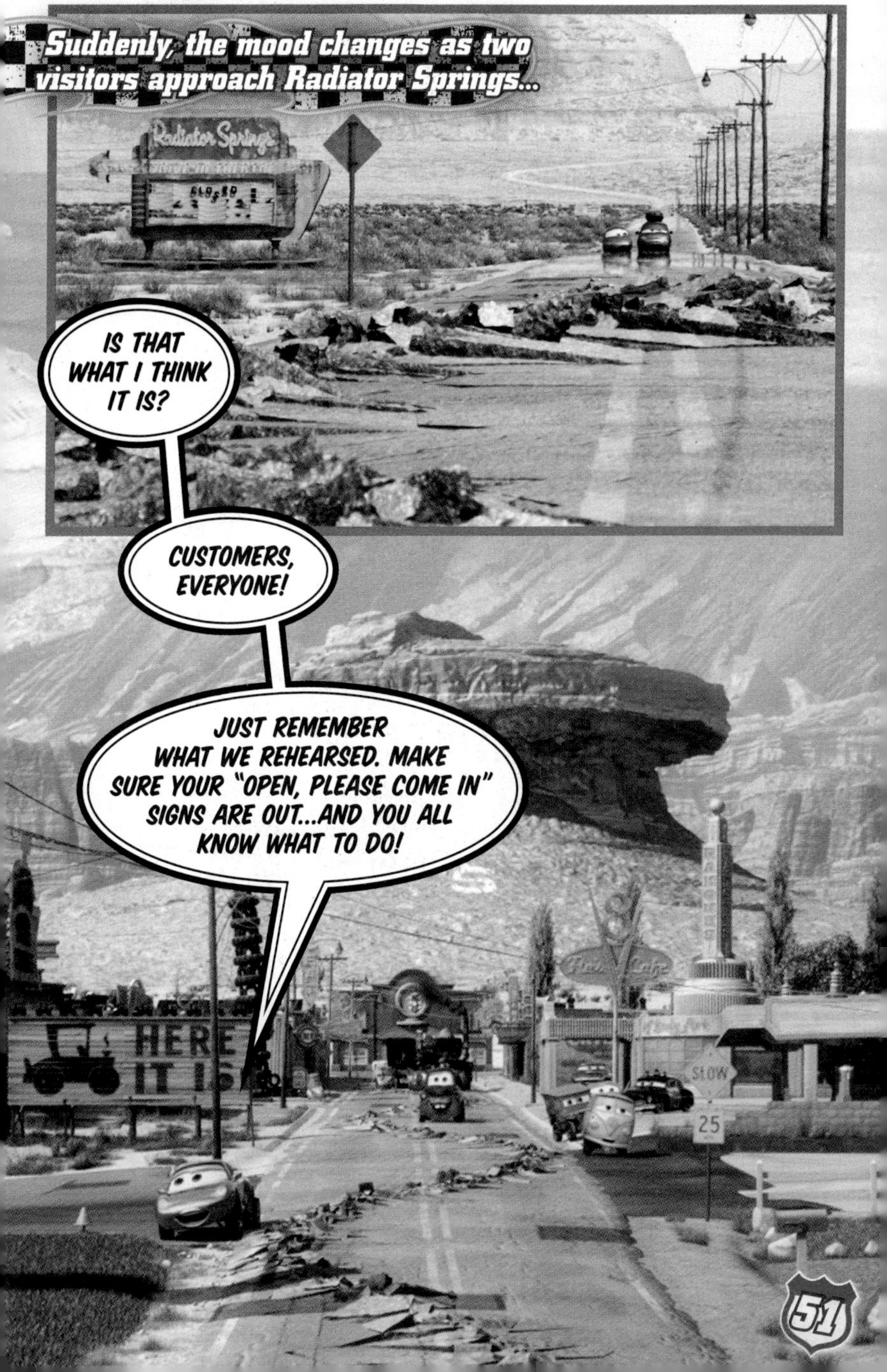
Suddenly, the mood changes as two visitors approach Radiator Springs...
Radiator Springs
IS THAT WHAT I THINK IT IS?
CUSTOMERS, EVERYONE!
JUST REMEMBER WHAT WE REHEARSED. MAKE SURE YOUR "OPEN, PLEASE COME IN" SIGNS ARE OUT...AND YOU ALL KNOW WHAT TO DO!
HERE IT IS
SLOW
25

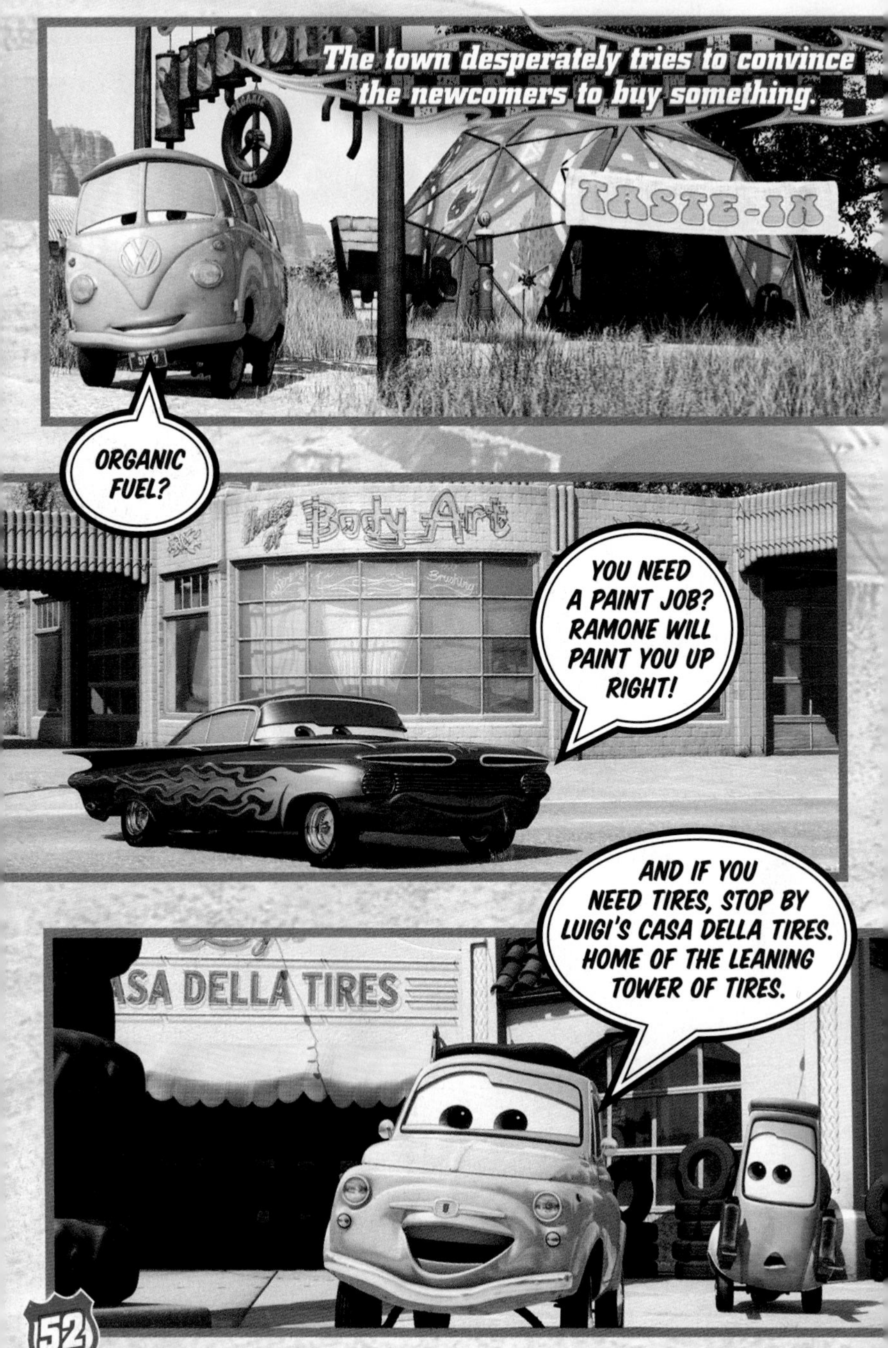
The town desperately tries to convince the newcomers to buy something.
TASTE-IN
ORGANIC FUEL?
Body Art
YOU NEED A PAINT JOB? RAMONE WILL PAINT YOU UP RIGHT!
AND IF YOU NEED TIRES, STOP BY LUIGI'S CASA DELLA TIRES. HOME OF THE LEANING TOWER OF TIRES.
ASA DELLA TIRES

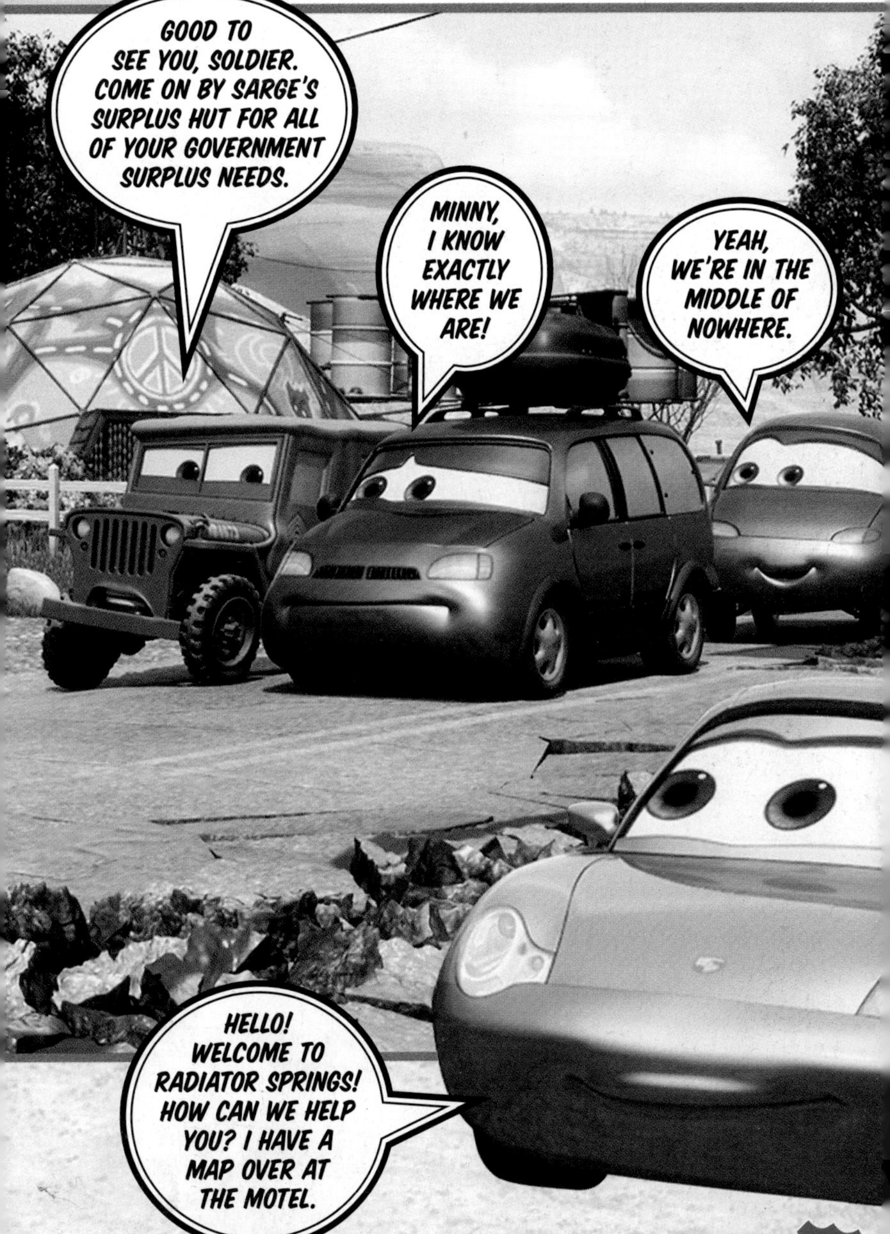
GOOD TO SEE YOU, SOLDIER. COME ON BY SARGE'S SURPLUS HUT FOR ALL OF YOUR GOVERNMENT SURPLUS NEEDS.
MINNY, I KNOW EXACTLY WHERE WE ARE!
YEAH, WE'RE IN THE MIDDLE OF NOWHERE.
HELLO! WELCOME TO RADIATOR SPRINGS! HOW CAN WE HELP YOU? I HAVE A MAP OVER AT THE MOTEL.

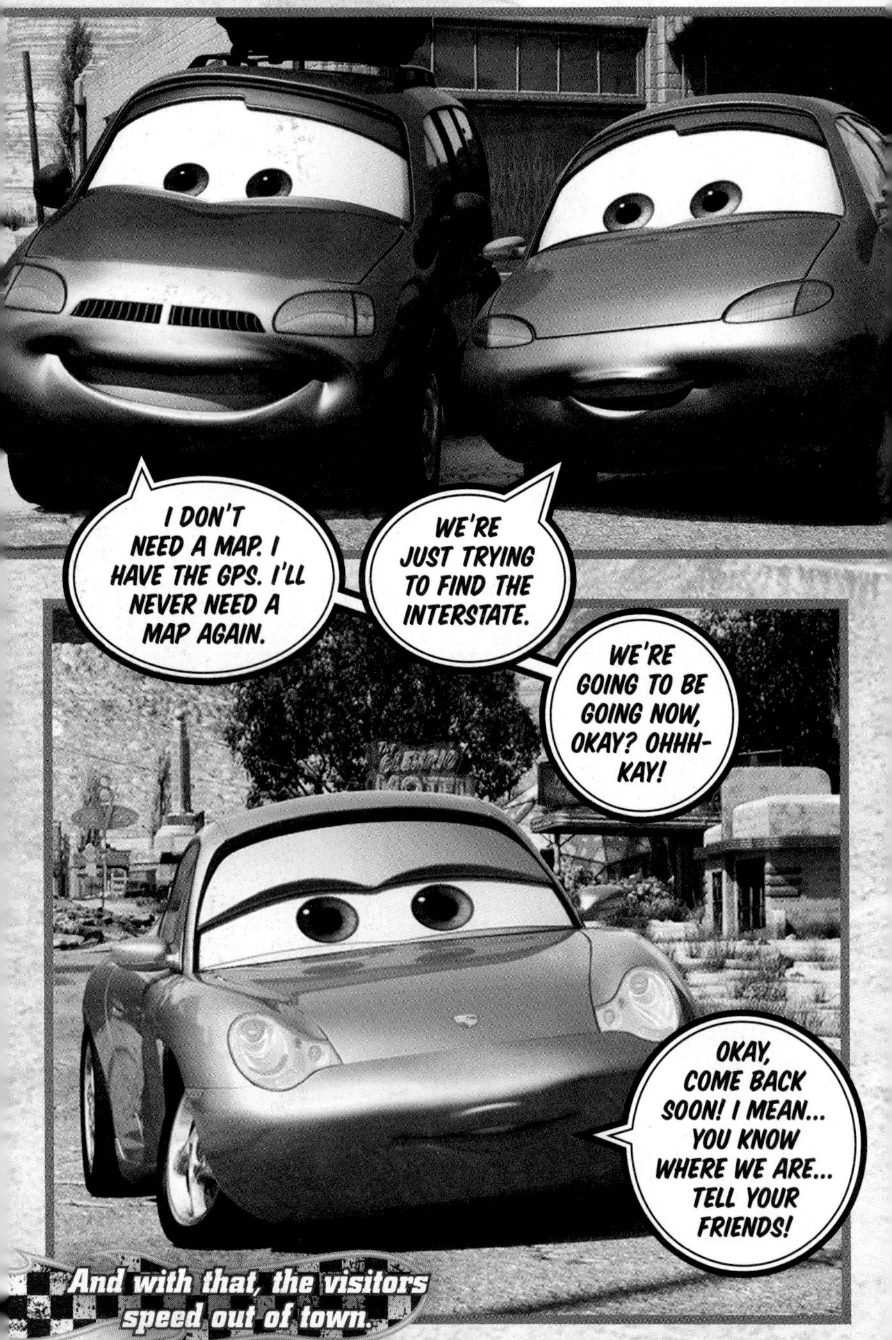
I DON'T NEED A MAP. I HAVE THE GPS. I'LL NEVER NEED A MAP AGAIN.
WE'RE JUST TRYING TO FIND THE INTERSTATE.
WE'RE GOING TO BE GOING NOW, OKAY? OHHH-KAY!
OKAY, COME BACK SOON! I MEAN... YOU KNOW WHERE WE ARE... TELL YOUR FRIENDS!
And with that, the visitors speed out of town.

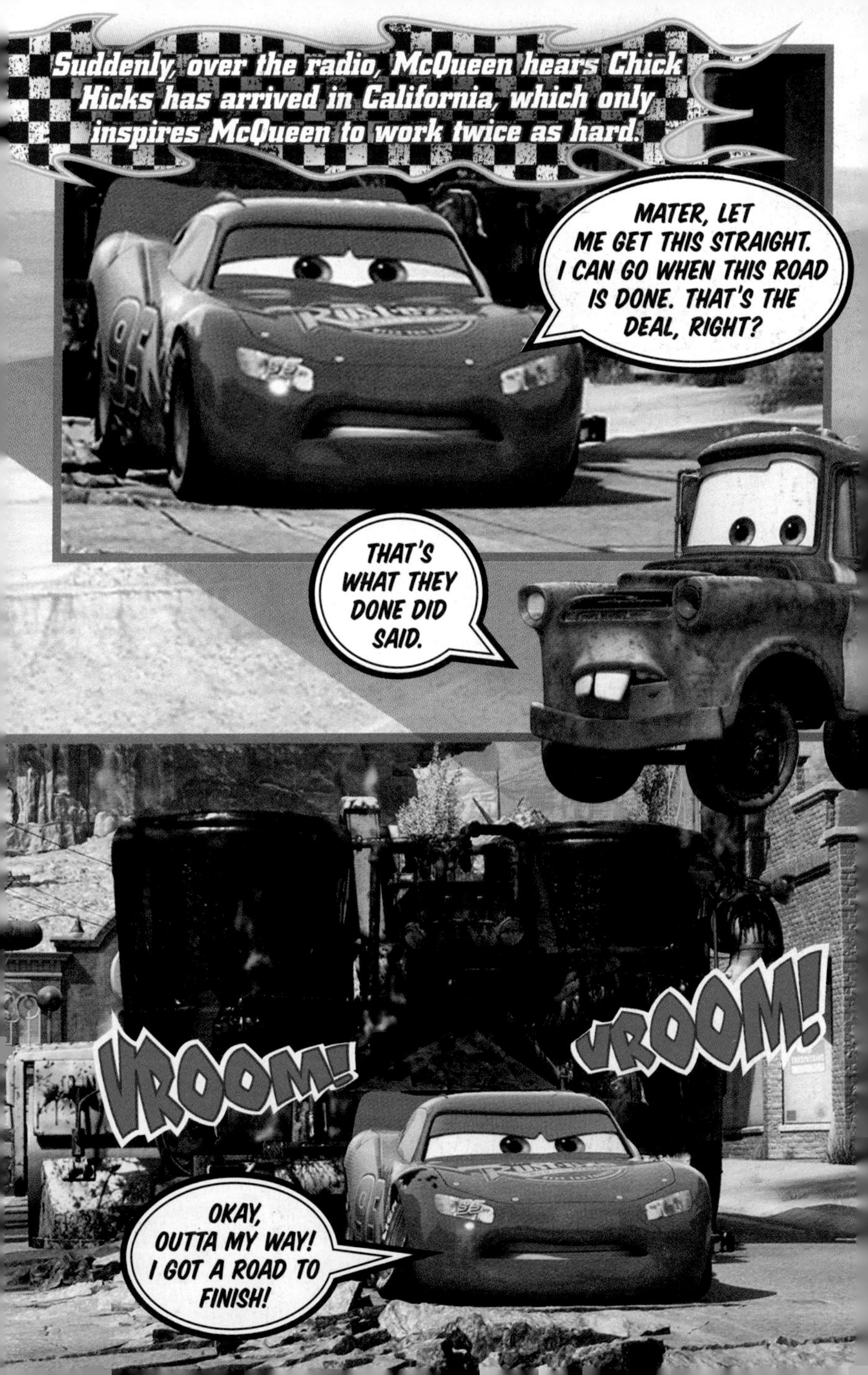
Suddenly, over the radio, McQueen hears Chick Hicks has arrived in California, which only inspires McQueen to work twice as hard.
MATER, LET ME GET THIS STRAIGHT. I CAN GO WHEN THIS ROAD IS DONE. THAT'S THE DEAL, RIGHT?
THAT'S WHAT THEY DONE DID SAID.
VROOM!
VROOM!
OKAY, OUTTA MY WAY! I GOT A ROAD TO FINISH!

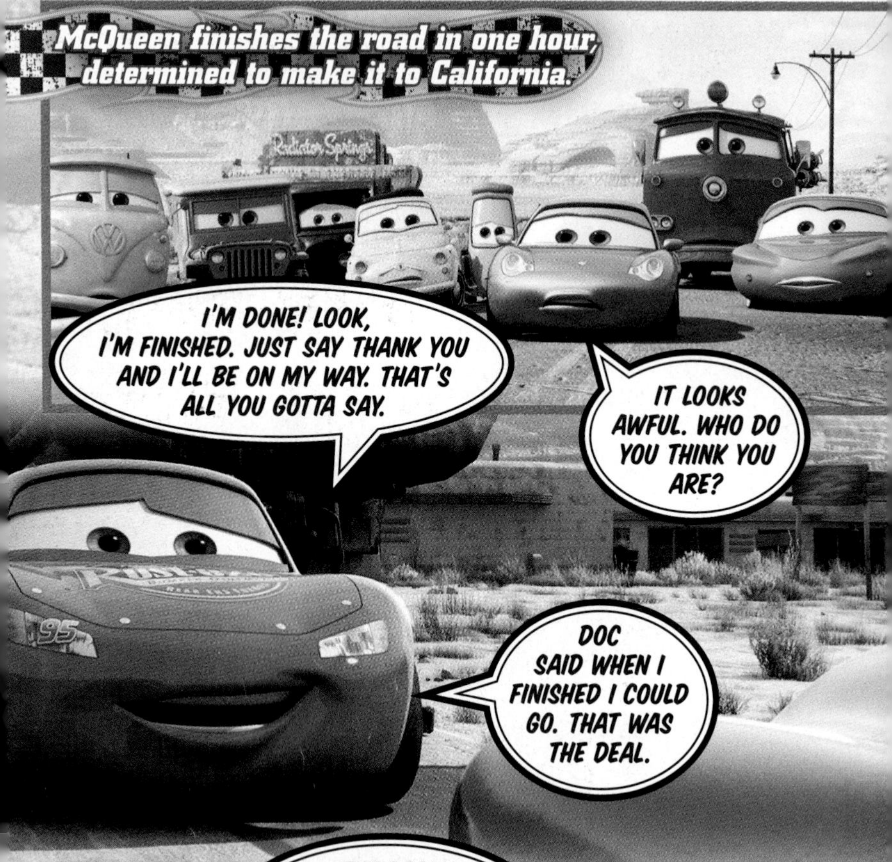
McQueen finishes the road in one hour, determined to make it to California.
Radiator Springs
I'M DONE! LOOK, I'M FINISHED. JUST SAY THANK YOU AND I'LL BE ON MY WAY. THAT'S ALL YOU GOTTA SAY.
IT LOOKS AWFUL. WHO DO YOU THINK YOU ARE?
DOC SAID WHEN I FINISHED I COULD GO. THAT WAS THE DEAL.
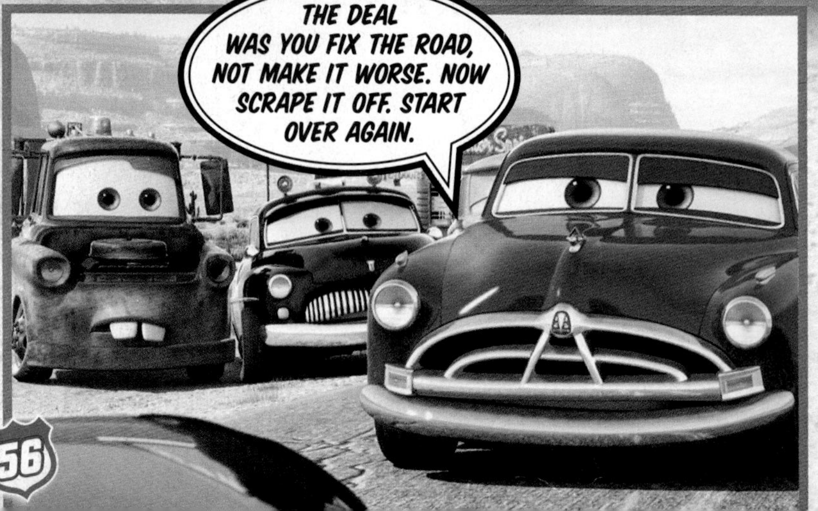
THE DEAL WAS YOU FIX THE ROAD, NOT MAKE IT WORSE. NOW SCRAPE IT OFF. START OVER AGAIN.

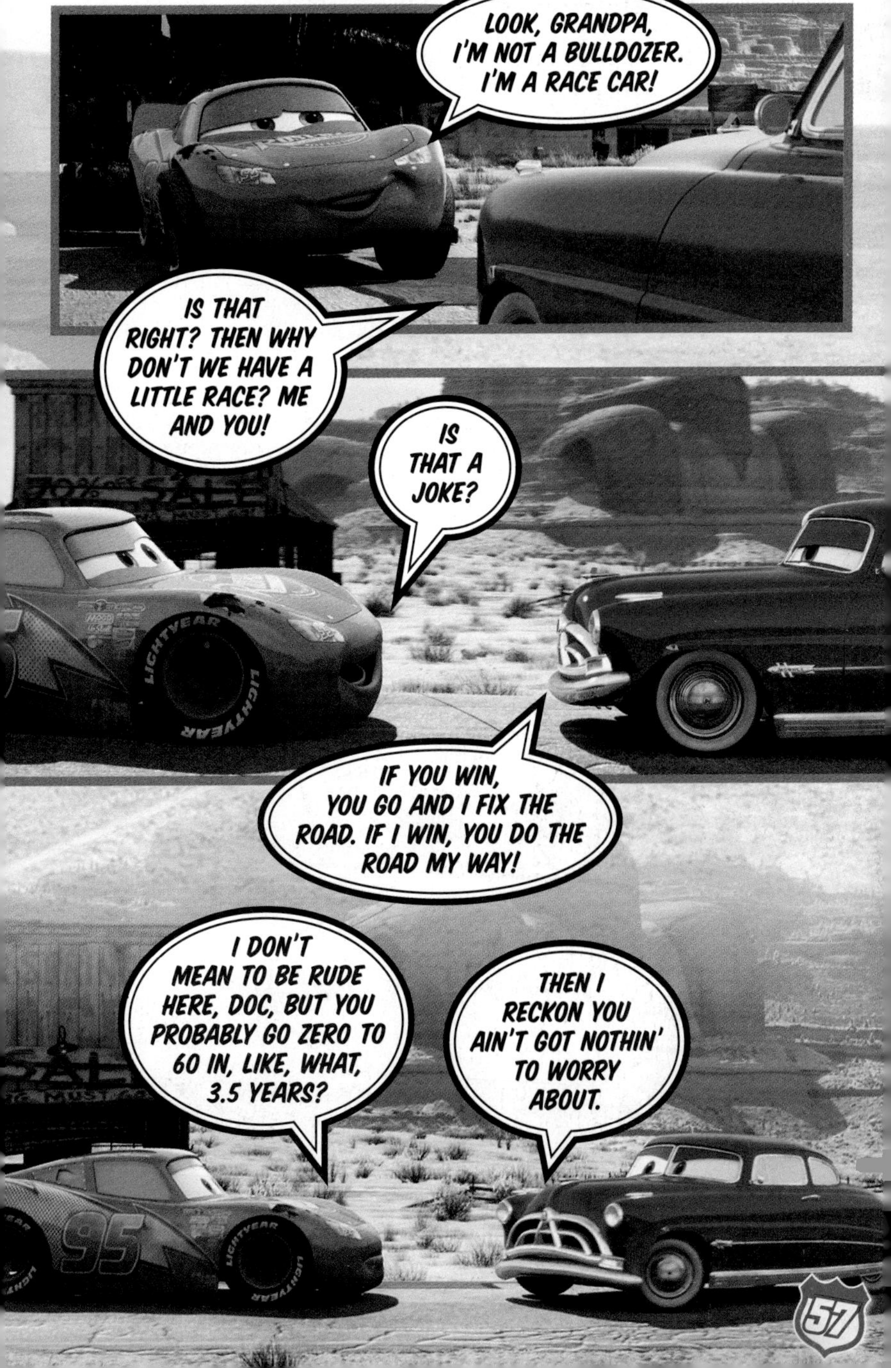
LOOK, GRANDPA, I'M NOT A BULLDOZER. I'M A RACE CAR!
IS THAT RIGHT? THEN WHY DON'T WE HAVE A LITTLE RACE? ME AND YOU!
IS THAT A JOKE?
IF YOU WIN, YOU GO AND I FIX THE ROAD. IF I WIN, YOU DO THE ROAD MY WAY!
I DON'T MEAN TO BE RUDE HERE, DOC, BUT YOU PROBABLY GO ZERO TO 60 IN, LIKE, WHAT, 3.5 YEARS?
THEN I RECKON YOU AIN'T GOT NOTHIN' TO WORRY ABOUT.

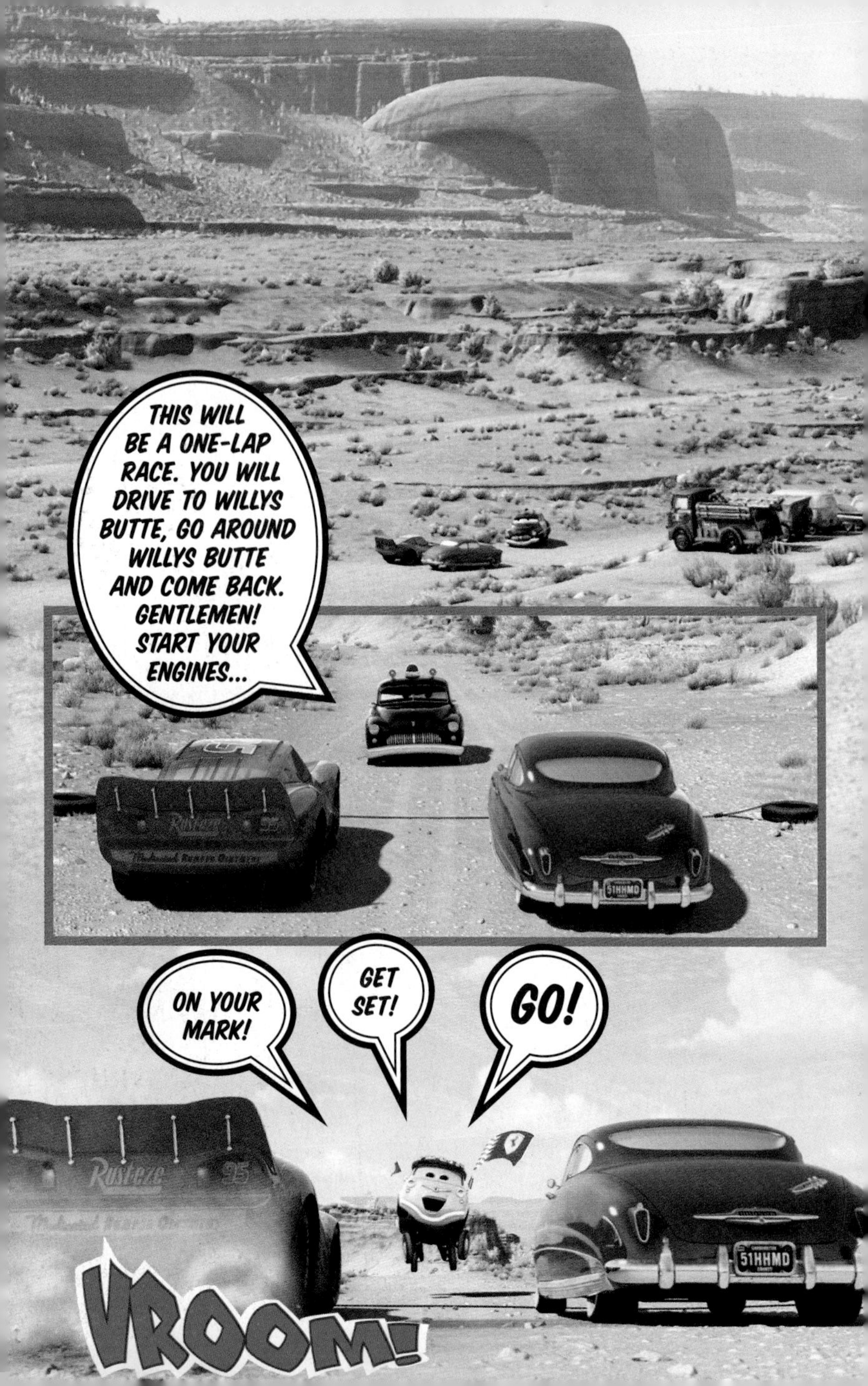
THIS WILL BE A ONE-LAP RACE. YOU WILL DRIVE TO WILLYS BUTTE, GO AROUND WILLYS BUTTE AND COME BACK. GENTLEMEN! START YOUR ENGINES...
ON YOUR MARK!
GET SET!
GO!
VROOM!

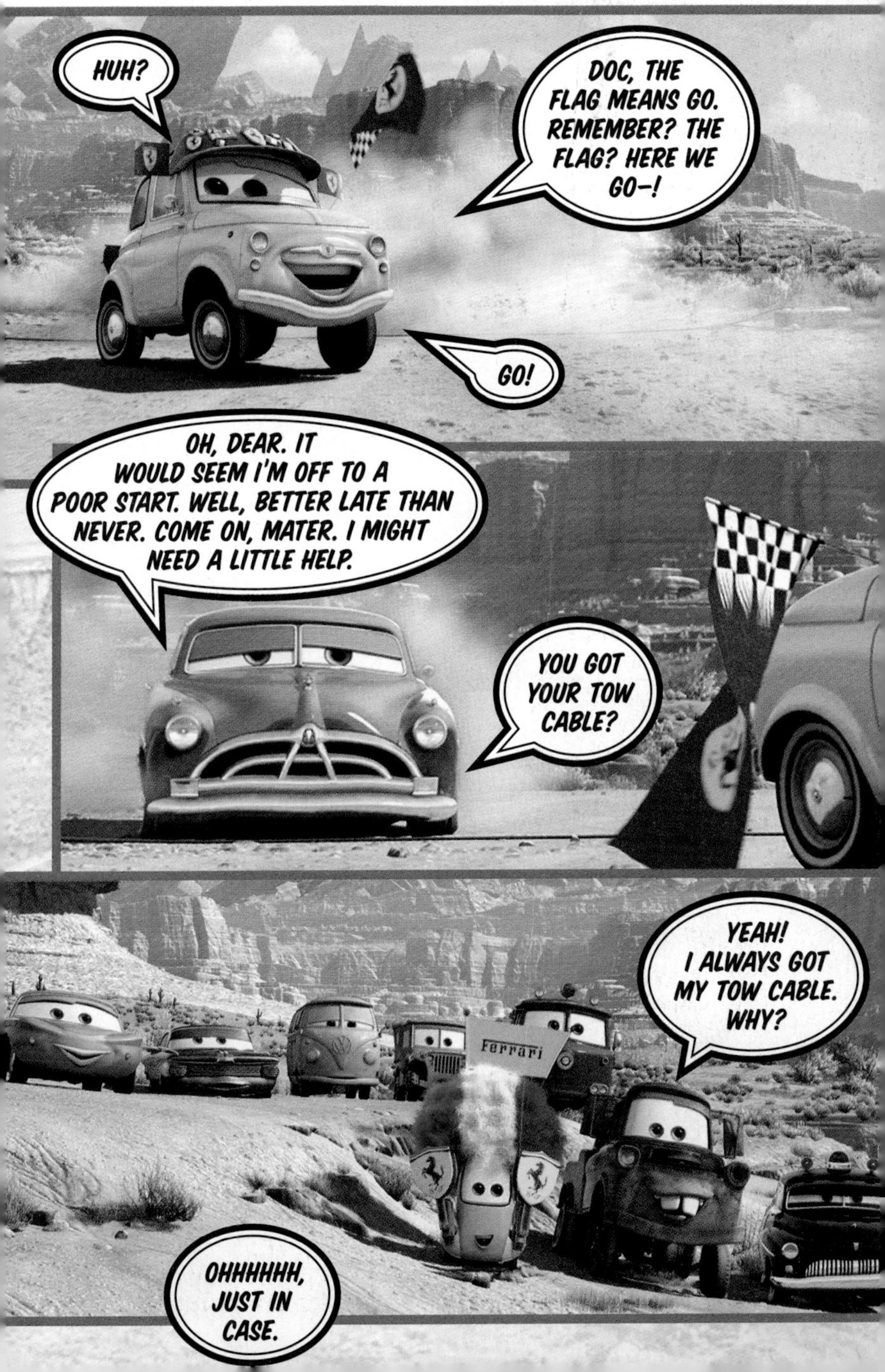
HUH?
DOC, THE FLAG MEANS GO. REMEMBER? THE FLAG? HERE WE GO–!
GO!
OH, DEAR. IT WOULD SEEM I'M OFF TO A POOR START. WELL, BETTER LATE THAN NEVER. COME ON, MATER. I MIGHT NEED A LITTLE HELP.
YOU GOT YOUR TOW CABLE?
YEAH! I ALWAYS GOT MY TOW CABLE. WHY?
OHHHHHH, JUST IN CASE.
Ferrari

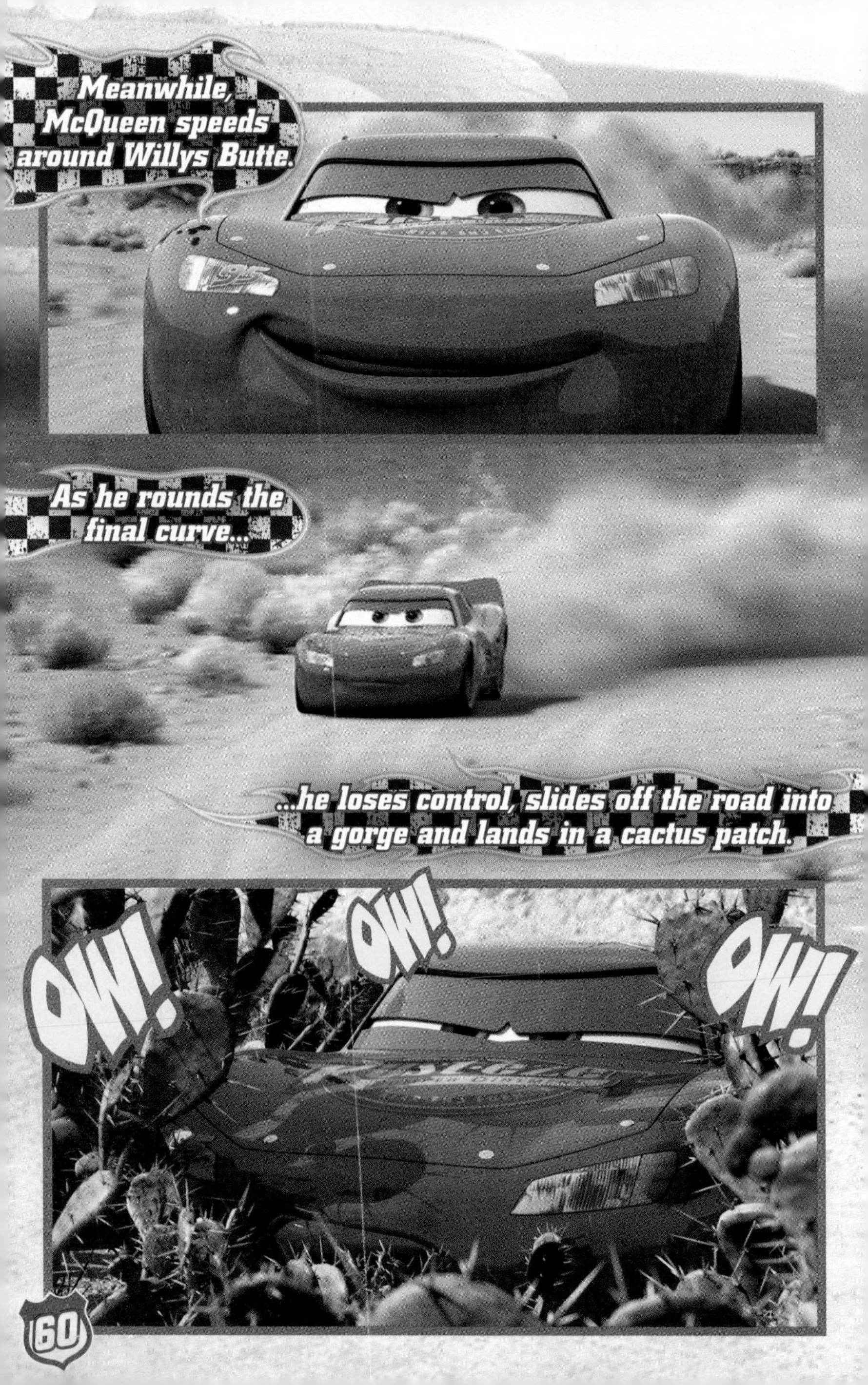
Meanwhile, McQueen speeds around Willys Butte.
As he rounds the final curve...
...he loses control, slides off the road into a gorge and lands in a cactus patch.
OW!
OW!
OW!

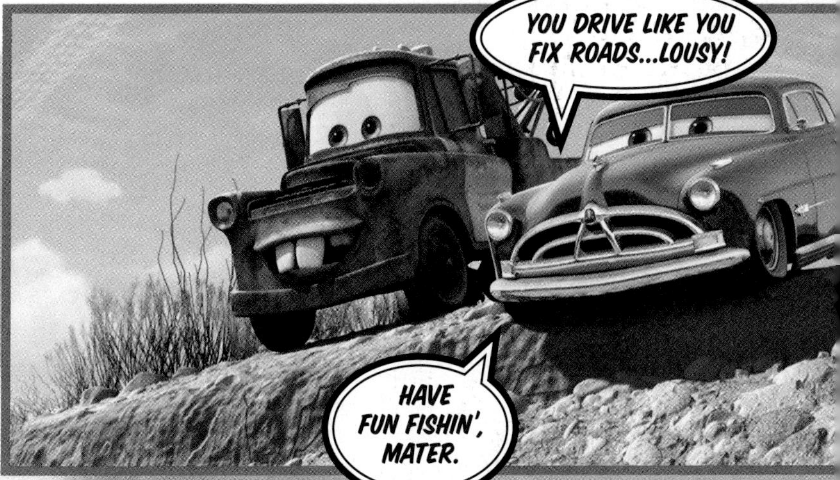
YOU DRIVE LIKE YOU FIX ROADS...LOUSY!
HAVE FUN FISHIN', MATER.

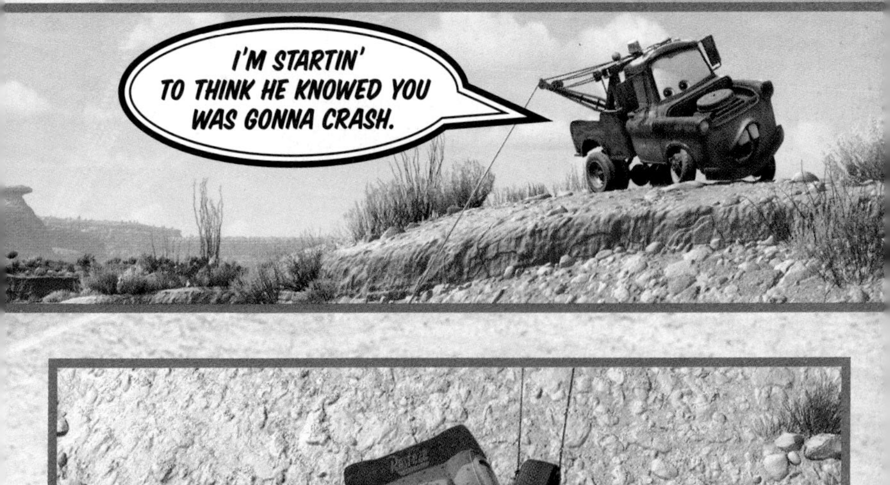
I'M STARTIN' TO THINK HE KNOWED YOU WAS GONNA CRASH.

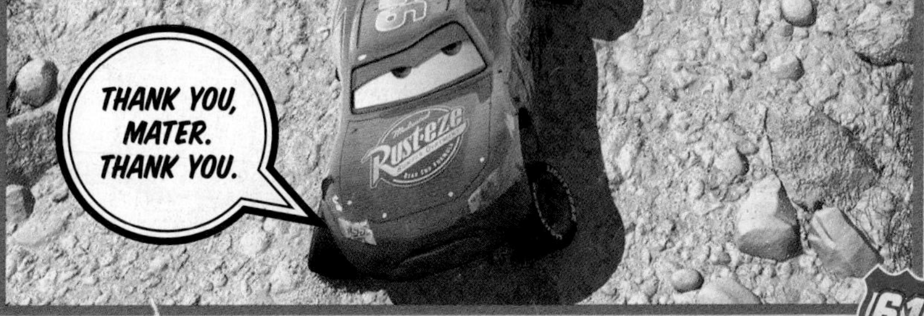
THANK YOU, MATER. THANK YOU.
Rust-eze

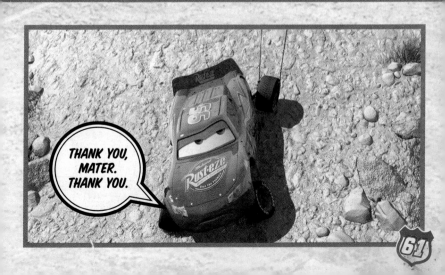

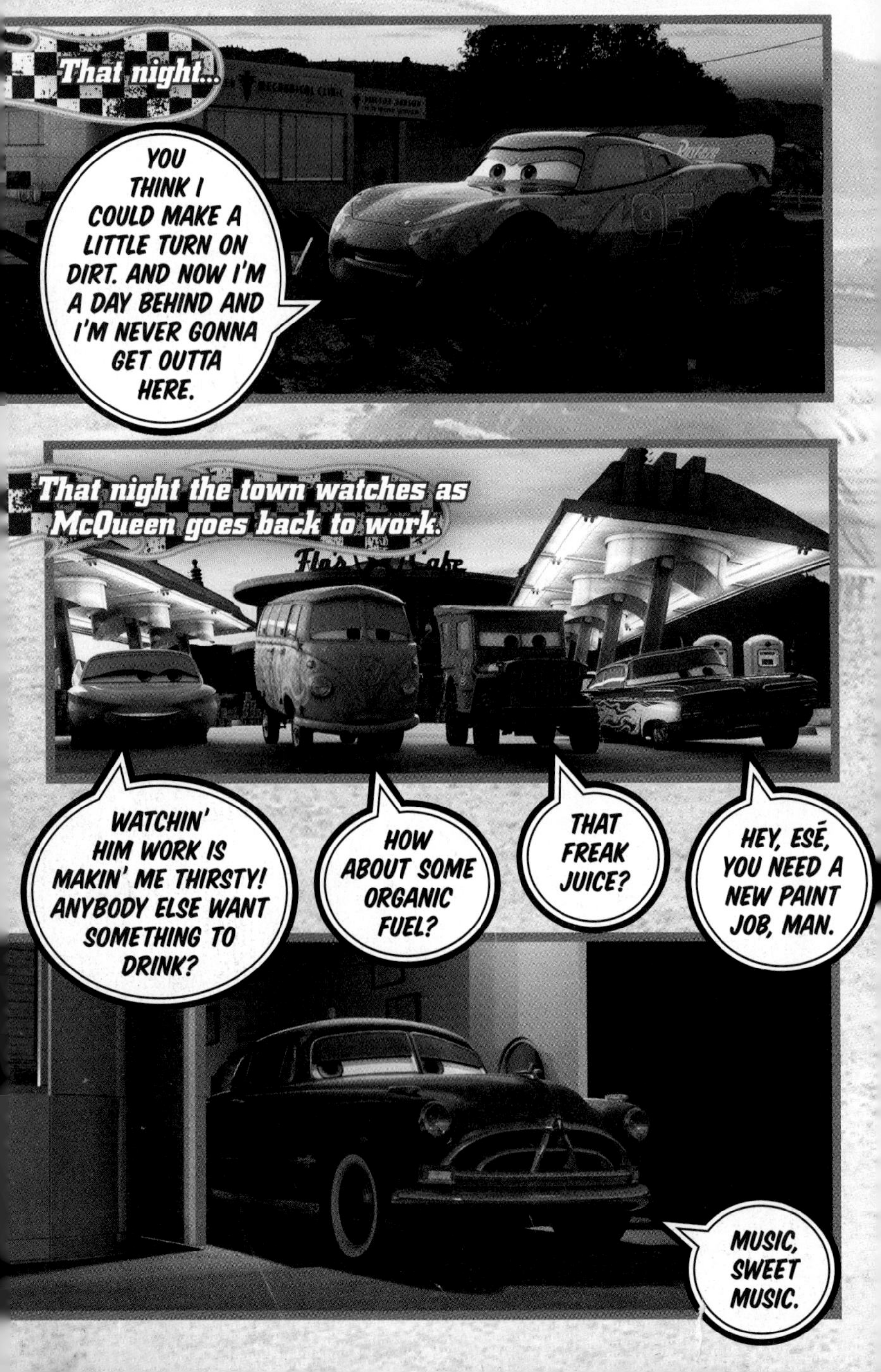
That night...
YOU THINK I COULD MAKE A LITTLE TURN ON DIRT. AND NOW I'M A DAY BEHIND AND I'M NEVER GONNA GET OUTTA HERE.
That night the town watches as McQueen goes back to work.
WATCHIN' HIM WORK IS MAKIN' ME THIRSTY! ANYBODY ELSE WANT SOMETHING TO DRINK?
HOW ABOUT SOME ORGANIC FUEL?
THAT FREAK JUICE?
HEY, ESÉ, YOU NEED A NEW PAINT JOB, MAN.
MUSIC, SWEET MUSIC.

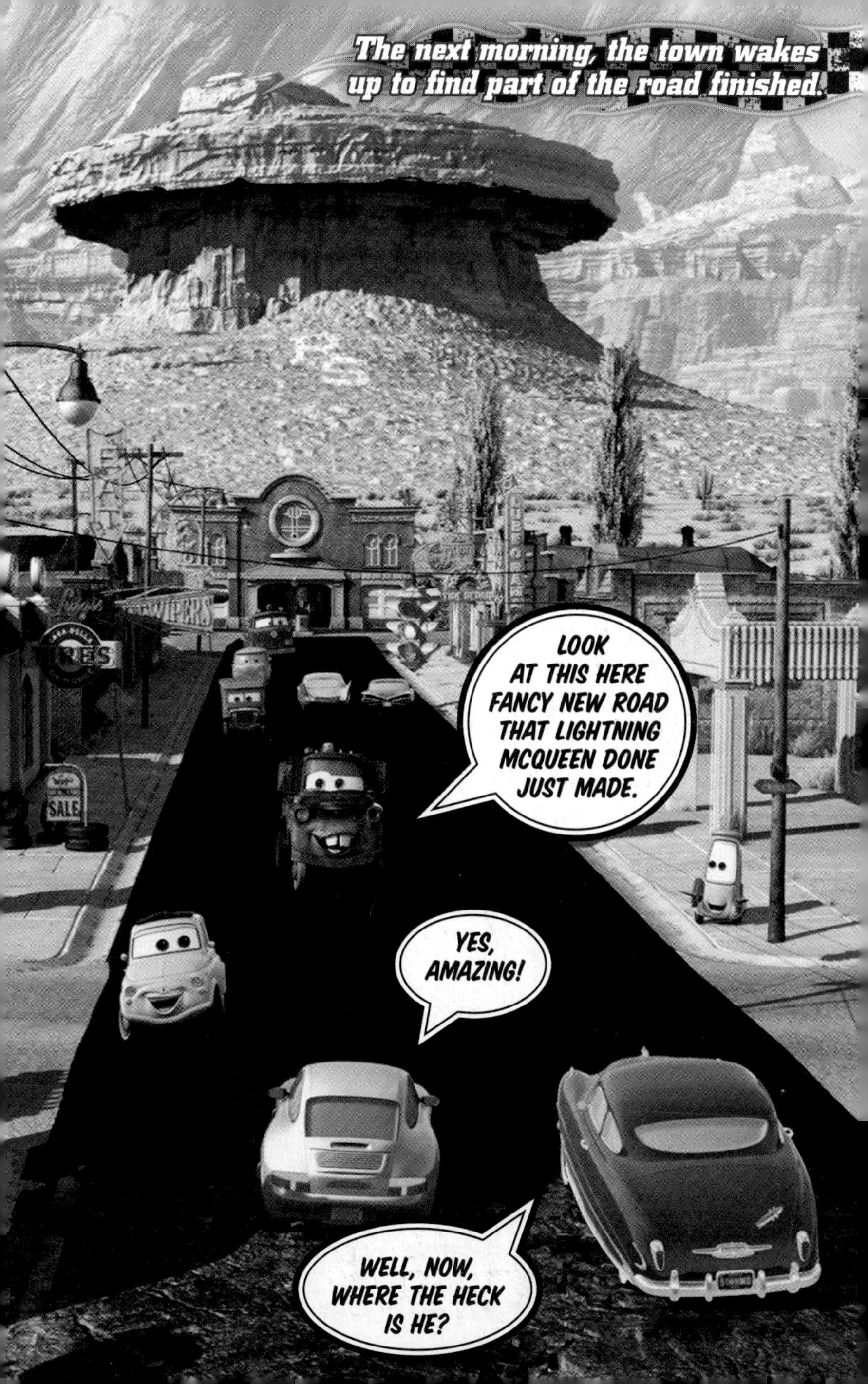
The next morning, the town wakes up to find part of the road finished.
LOOK AT THIS HERE FANCY NEW ROAD THAT LIGHTNING MCQUEEN DONE JUST MADE.
YES, AMAZING!
WELL, NOW, WHERE THE HECK IS HE?

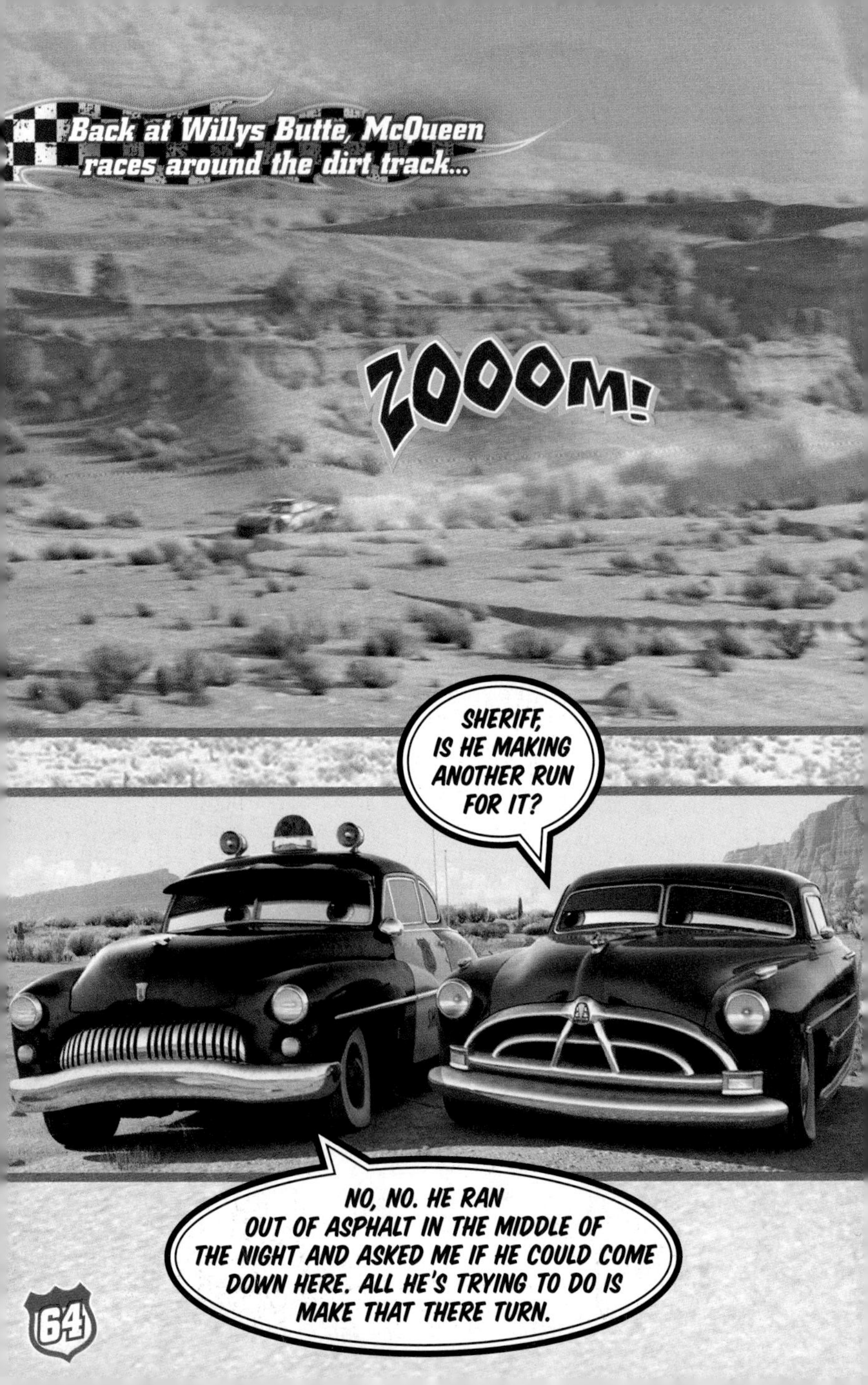
Back at Willys Butte, McQueen races around the dirt track...
ZOOOM!
SHERIFF, IS HE MAKING ANOTHER RUN FOR IT?
NO, NO. HE RAN OUT OF ASPHALT IN THE MIDDLE OF THE NIGHT AND ASKED ME IF HE COULD COME DOWN HERE. ALL HE'S TRYING TO DO IS MAKE THAT THERE TURN.

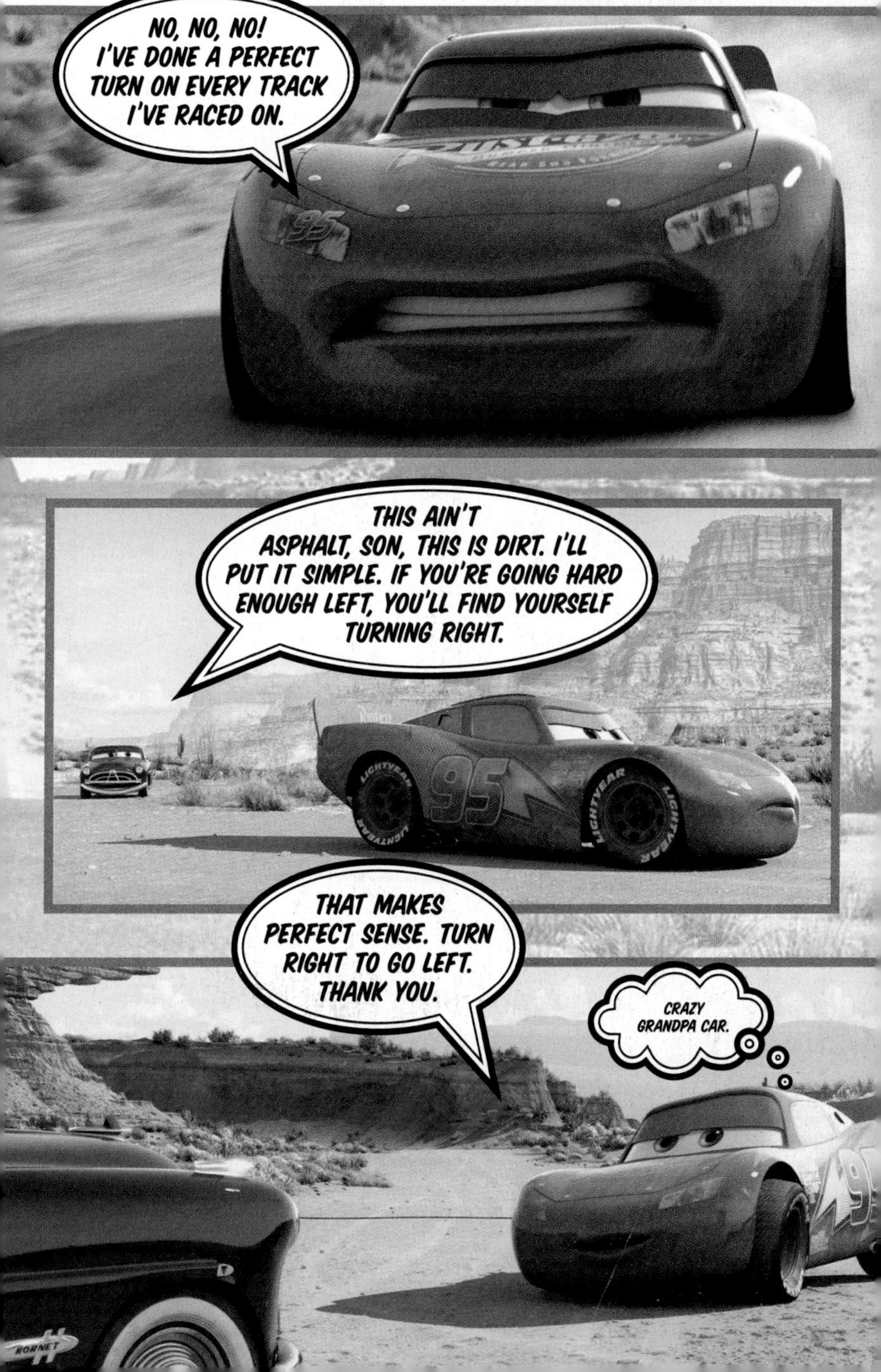
NO, NO, NO! I'VE DONE A PERFECT TURN ON EVERY TRACK I'VE RACED ON.
THIS AIN'T ASPHALT, SON, THIS IS DIRT. I'LL PUT IT SIMPLE. IF YOU'RE GOING HARD ENOUGH LEFT, YOU'LL FIND YOURSELF TURNING RIGHT.
THAT MAKES PERFECT SENSE. TURN RIGHT TO GO LEFT. THANK YOU.
CRAZY GRANDPA CAR.

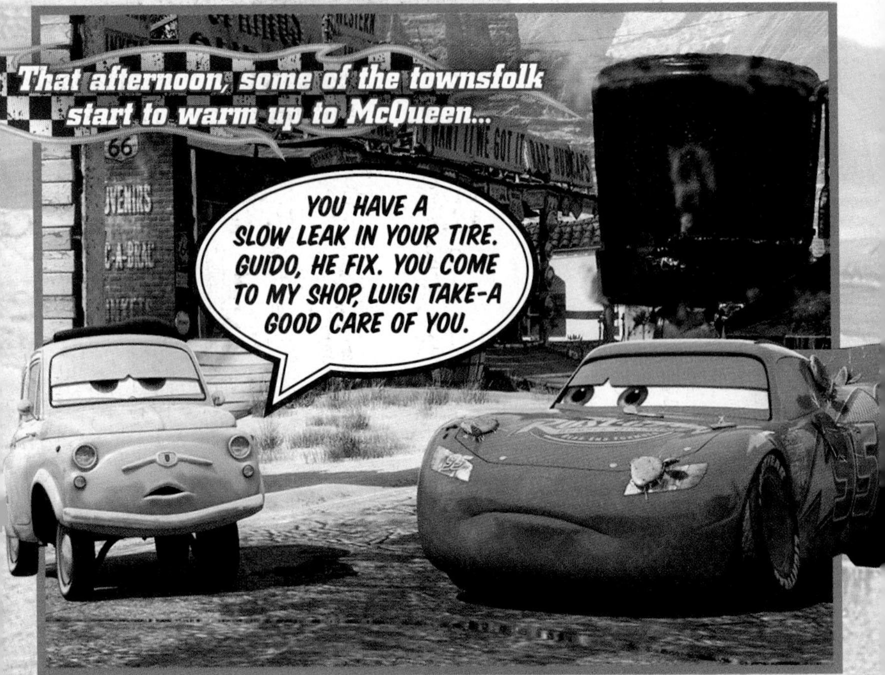
That afternoon, some of the townsfolk start to warm up to McQueen...
YOU HAVE A SLOW LEAK IN YOUR TIRE. GUIDO, HE FIX. YOU COME TO MY SHOP, LUIGI TAKE-A GOOD CARE OF YOU.

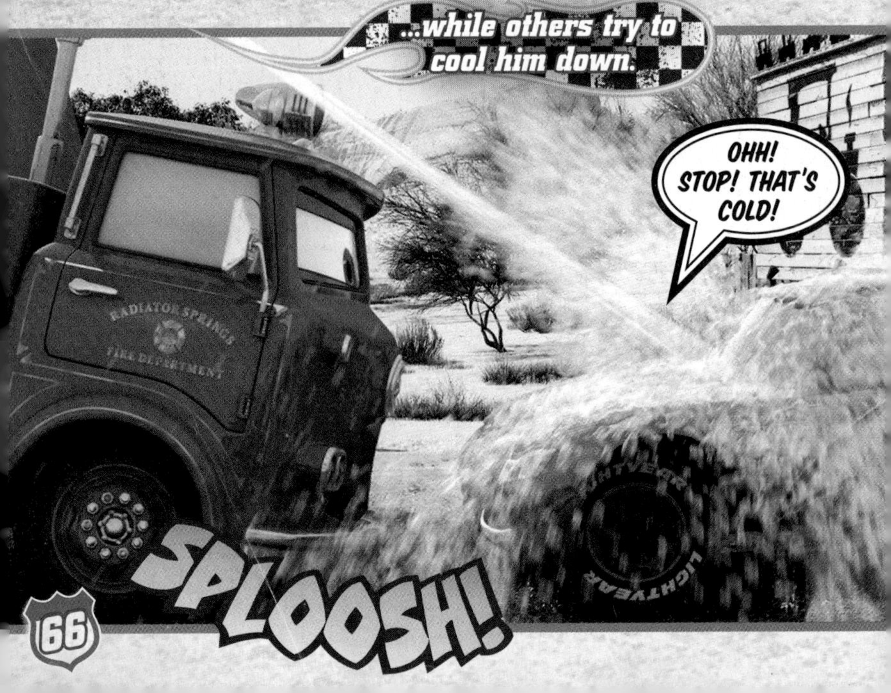
...while others try to cool him down.
OHH! STOP! THAT'S COLD!
SPLOOSH!

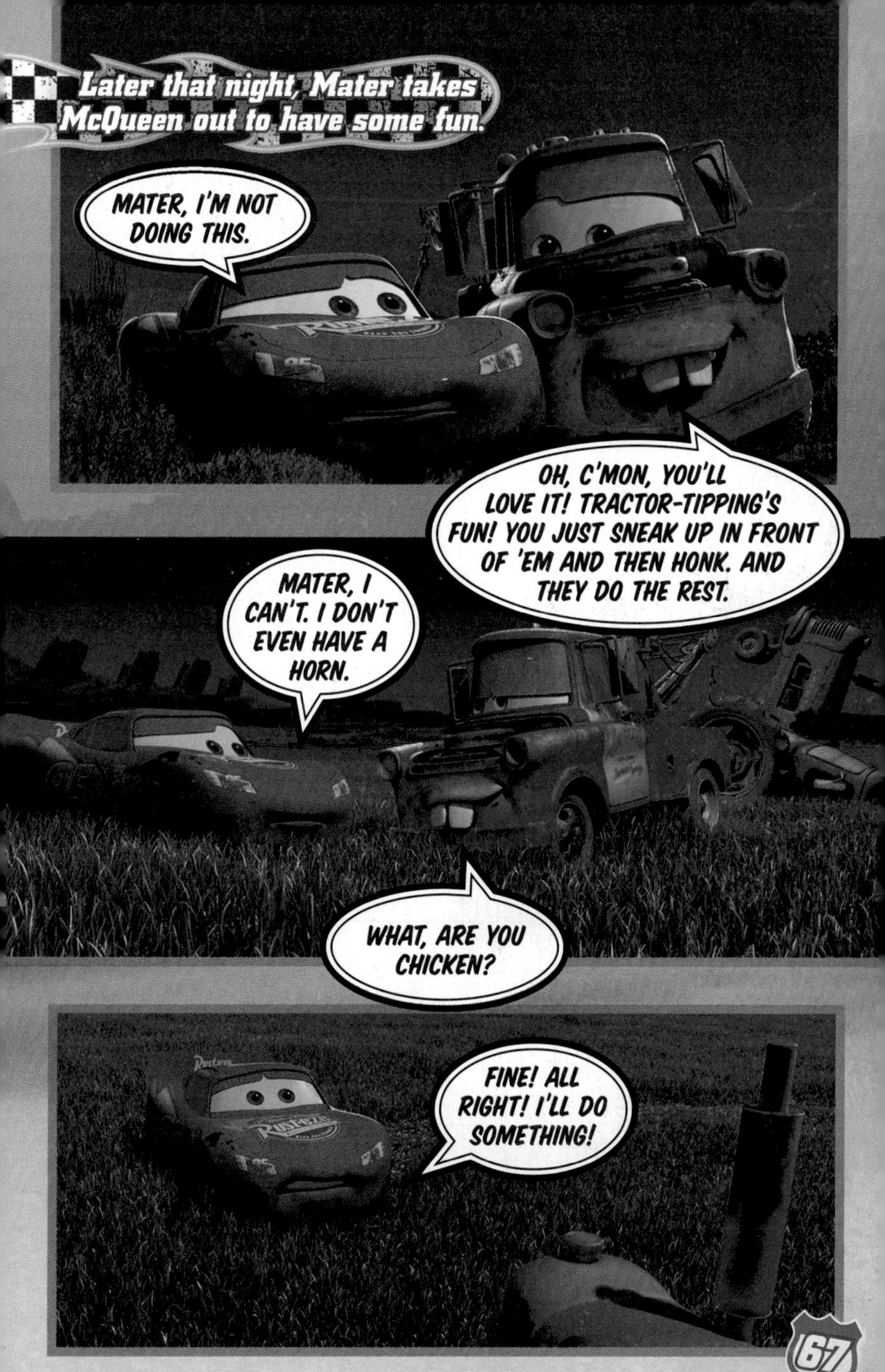
Later that night, Mater takes McQueen out to have some fun.
MATER, I'M NOT DOING THIS.
OH, C'MON, YOU'LL LOVE IT! TRACTOR-TIPPING'S FUN! YOU JUST SNEAK UP IN FRONT OF 'EM AND THEN HONK. AND THEY DO THE REST.
MATER, I CAN'T. I DON'T EVEN HAVE A HORN.
WHAT, ARE YOU CHICKEN?
FINE! ALL RIGHT! I'LL DO SOMETHING!

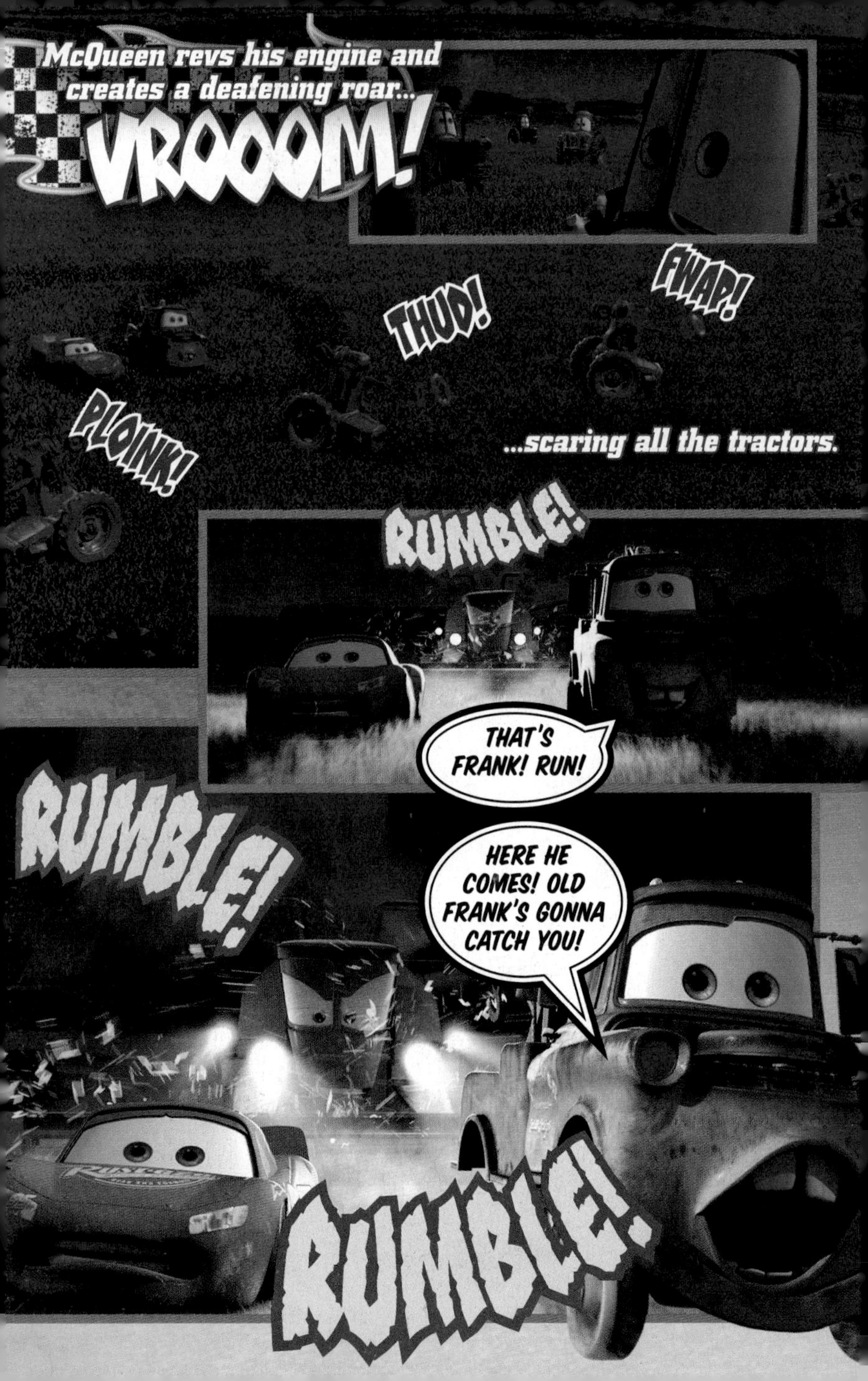
McQueen revs his engine and creates a deafening roar...
VROOOM!
THUD!
FWAP!
PLOINK!
...scaring all the tractors.
RUMBLE!
THAT'S FRANK! RUN!
RUMBLE!
HERE HE COMES! OLD FRANK'S GONNA CATCH YOU!
RUMBLE!

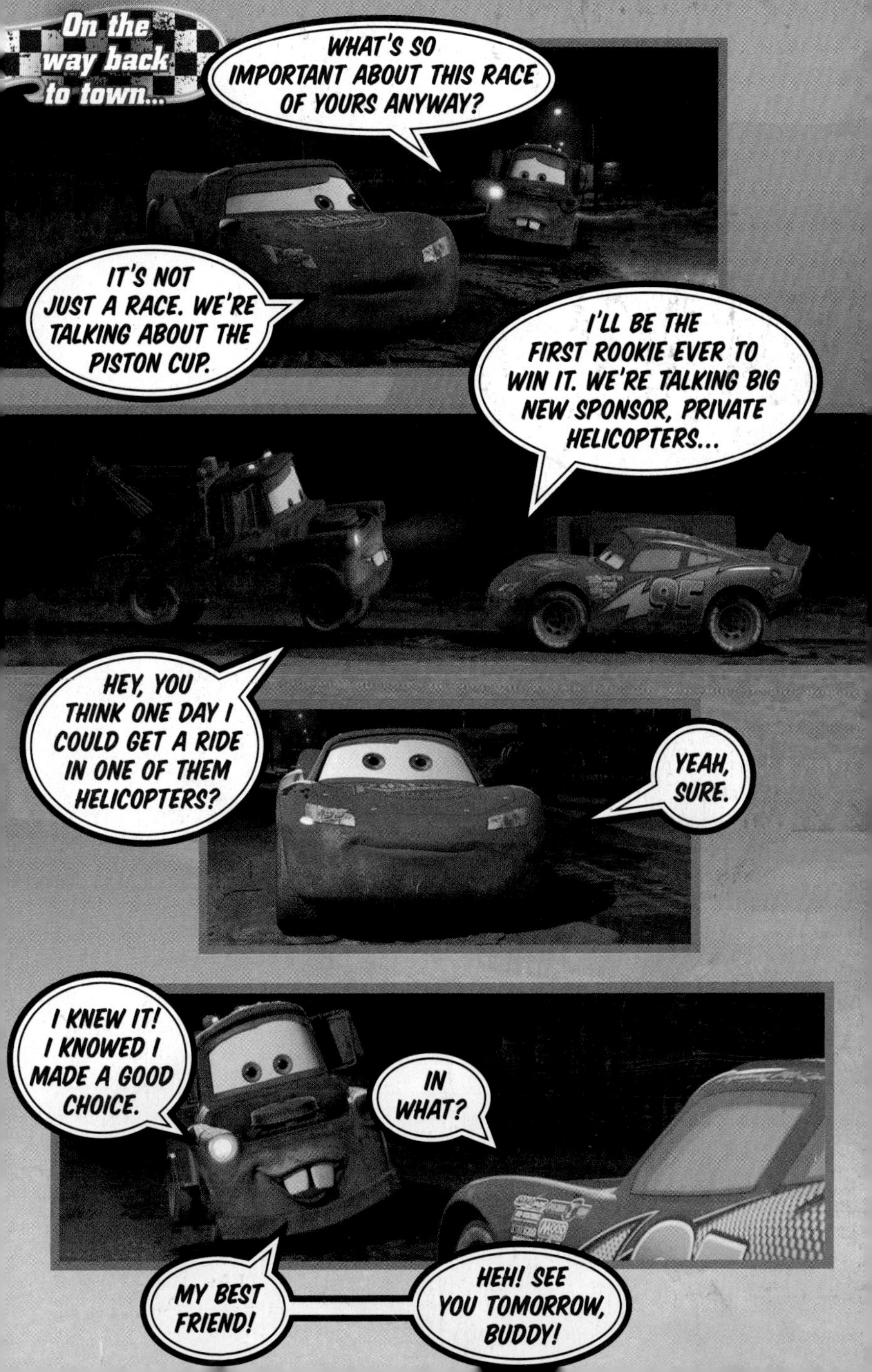

On the way back to town...
WHAT'S SO IMPORTANT ABOUT THIS RACE OF YOURS ANYWAY?
IT'S NOT JUST A RACE. WE'RE TALKING ABOUT THE PISTON CUP.
I'LL BE THE FIRST ROOKIE EVER TO WIN IT. WE'RE TALKING BIG NEW SPONSOR, PRIVATE HELICOPTERS...
HEY, YOU THINK ONE DAY I COULD GET A RIDE IN ONE OF THEM HELICOPTERS?
YEAH, SURE.
I KNEW IT! I KNOWED I MADE A GOOD CHOICE.
IN WHAT?
MY BEST FRIEND!
HEH! SEE YOU TOMORROW, BUDDY!

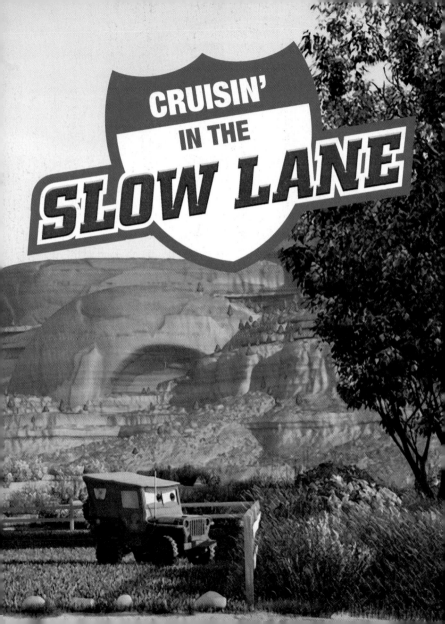

CRUISIN'
IN THE
SLOW LANE

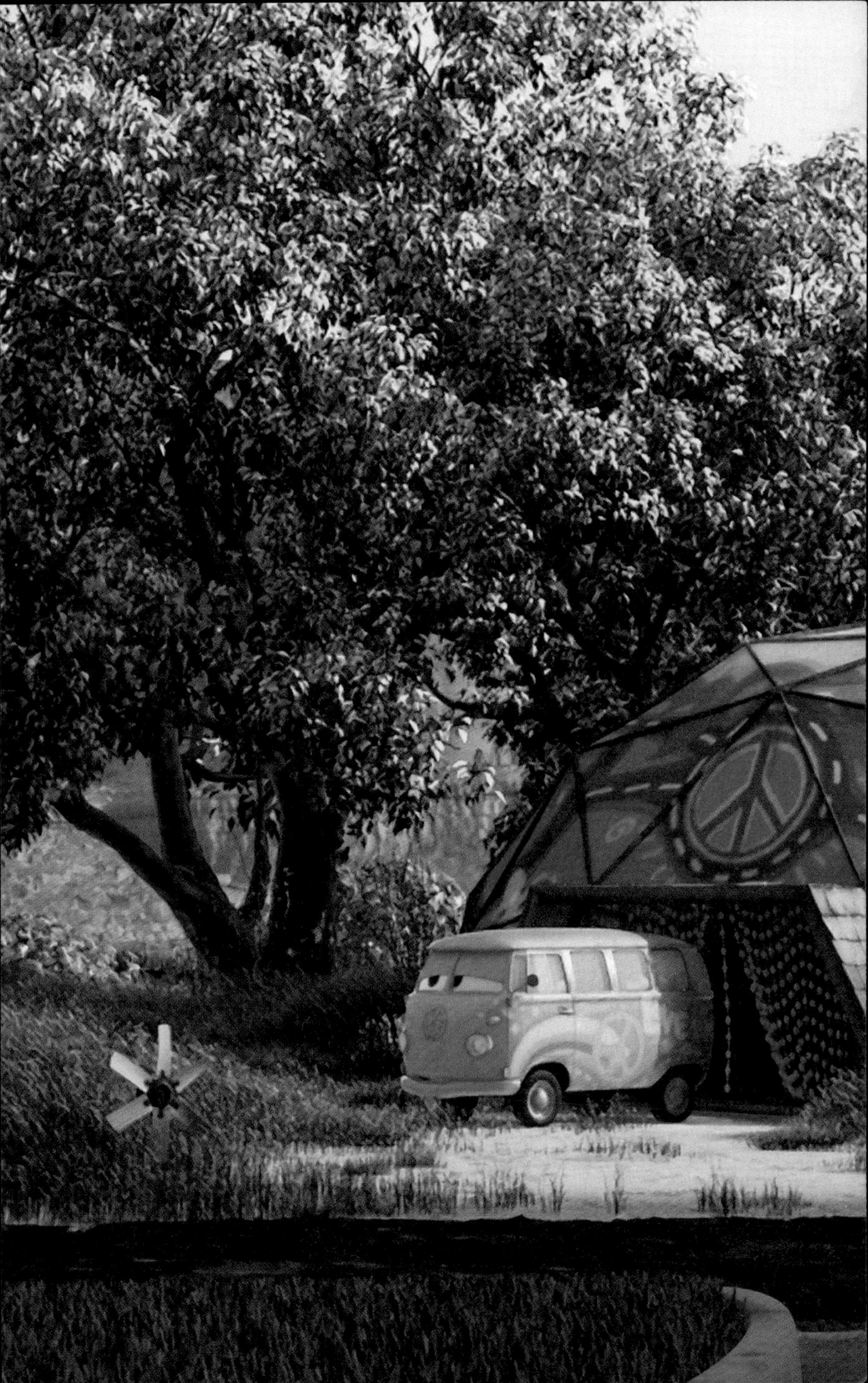

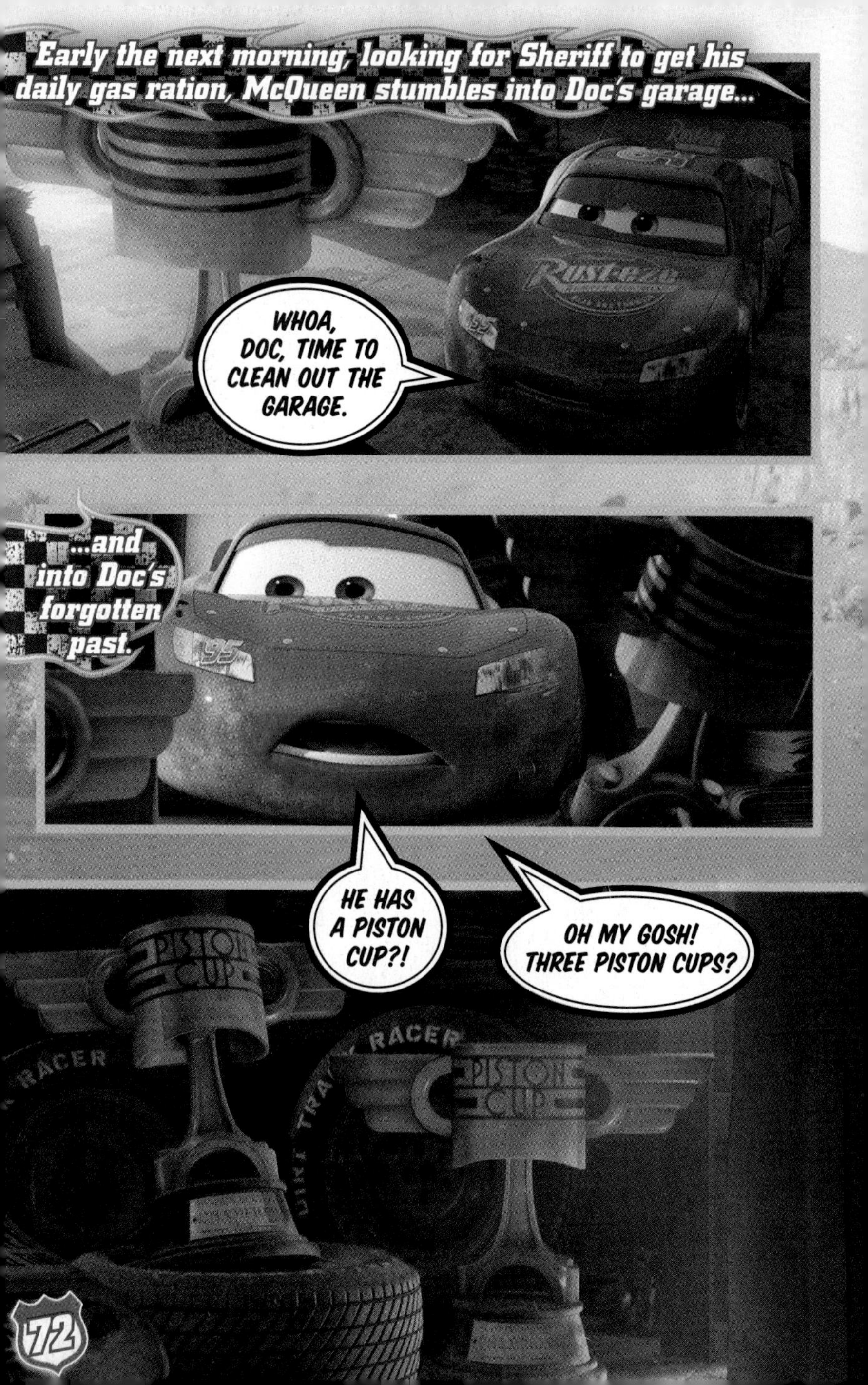
Early the next morning, looking for Sheriff to get his daily gas ration, McQueen stumbles into Doc's garage...
WHOA, DOC, TIME TO CLEAN OUT THE GARAGE.
...and into Doc's forgotten past.
HE HAS A PISTON CUP?!
OH MY GOSH! THREE PISTON CUPS?
PISTON CUP
RACER
PISTON CUP
RACER

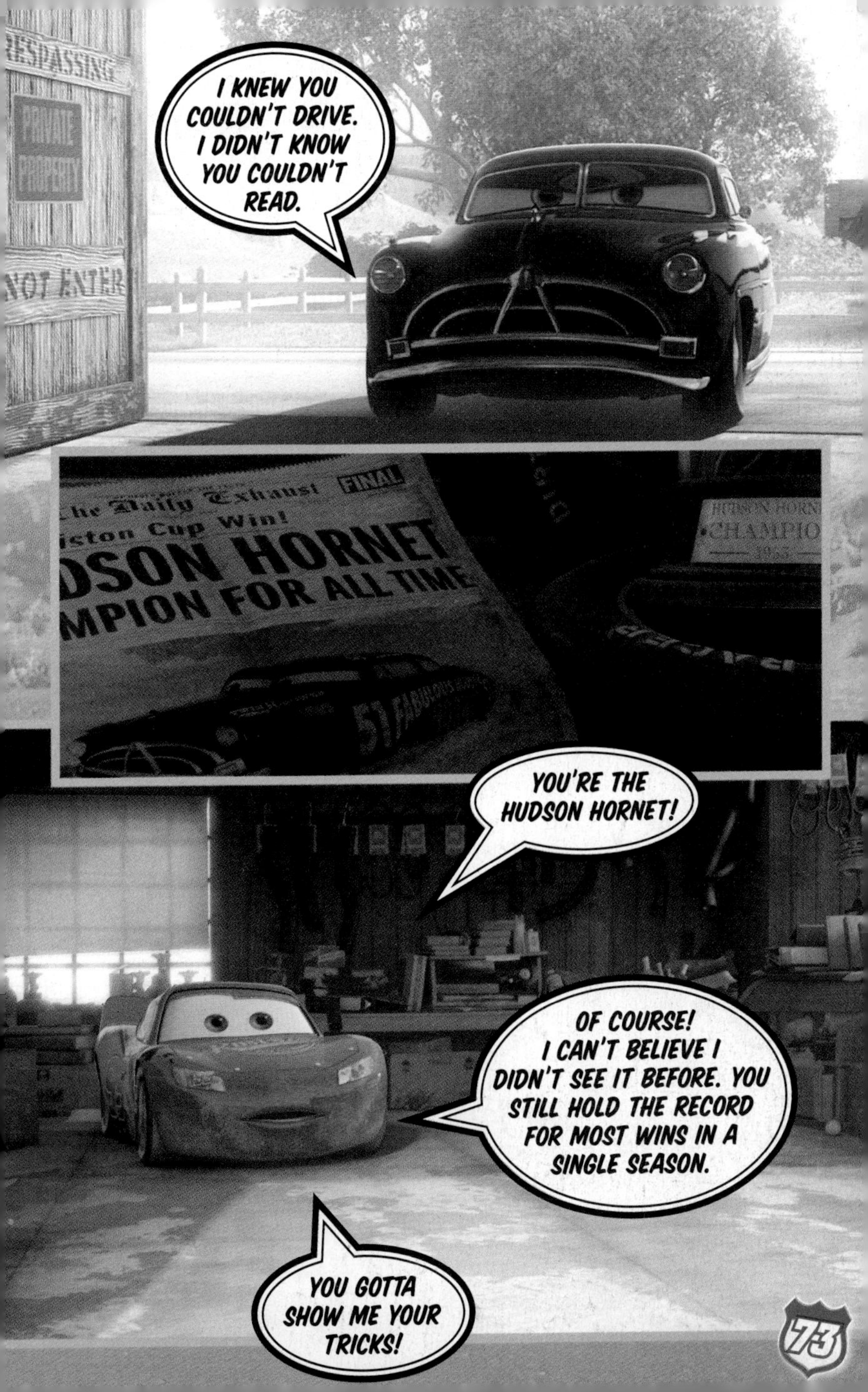
I KNEW YOU COULDN'T DRIVE. I DIDN'T KNOW YOU COULDN'T READ.
FINAL
YOU'RE THE HUDSON HORNET!
OF COURSE! I CAN'T BELIEVE I DIDN'T SEE IT BEFORE. YOU STILL HOLD THE RECORD FOR MOST WINS IN A SINGLE SEASON.
YOU GOTTA SHOW ME YOUR TRICKS!

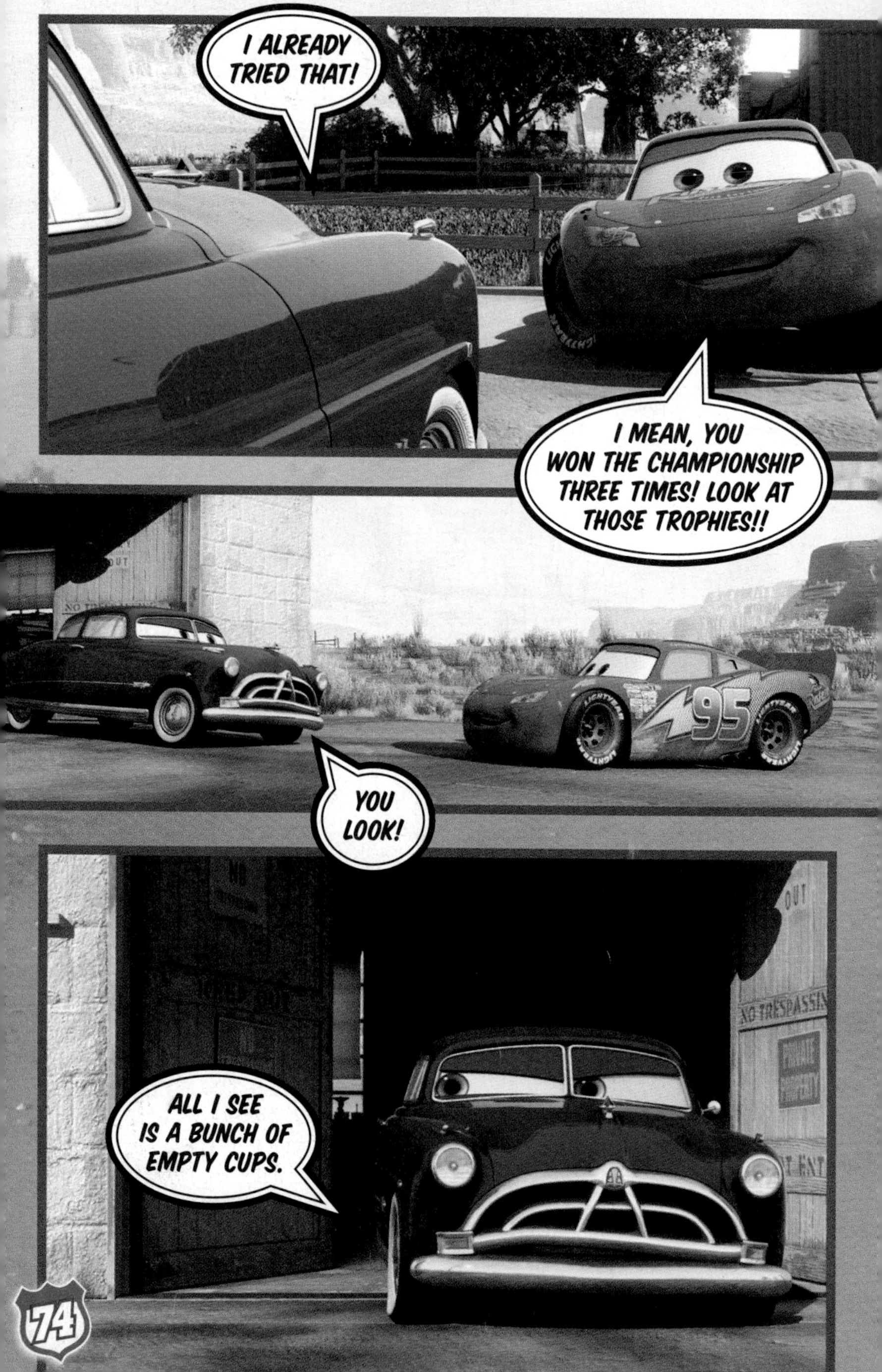
I ALREADY TRIED THAT!
I MEAN, YOU WON THE CHAMPIONSHIP THREE TIMES! LOOK AT THOSE TROPHIES!!
YOU LOOK!
ALL I SEE IS A BUNCH OF EMPTY CUPS.

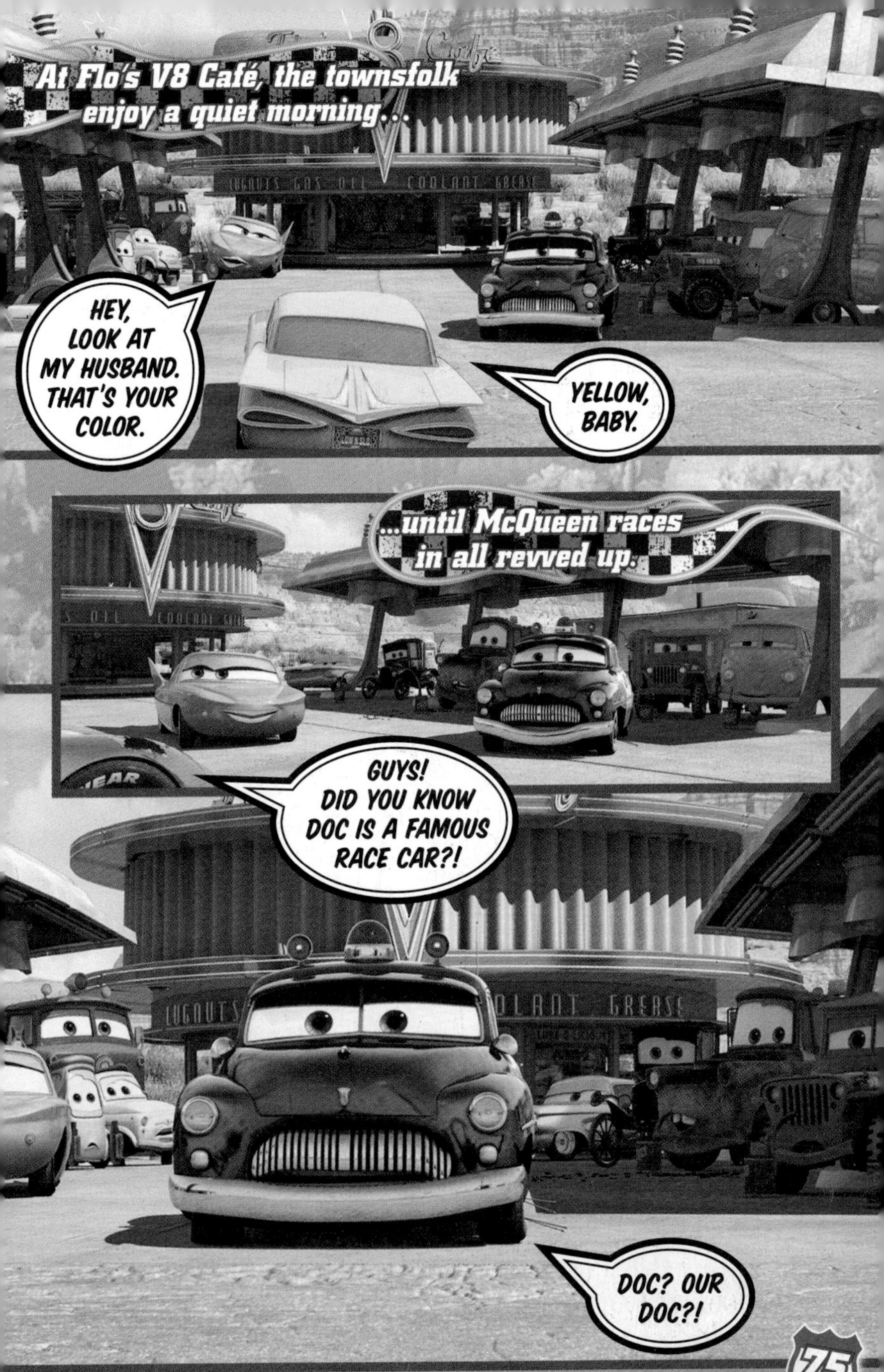
At Flo's V8 Café, the townsfolk enjoy a quiet morning...
HEY, LOOK AT MY HUSBAND. THAT'S YOUR COLOR.
YELLOW, BABY.
...until McQueen races in all revved up.
GUYS! DID YOU KNOW DOC IS A FAMOUS RACE CAR?!
DOC? OUR DOC?!

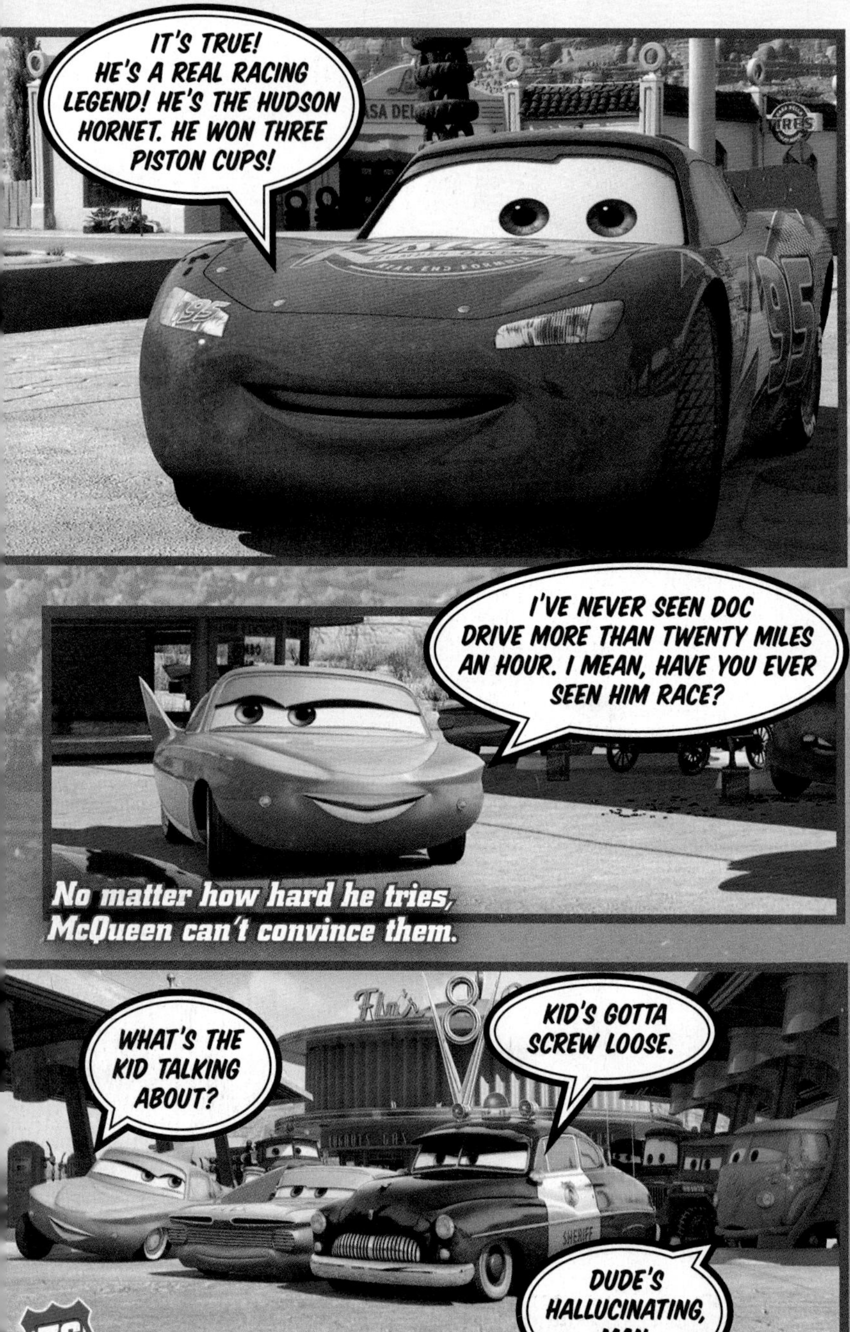
IT'S TRUE! HE'S A REAL RACING LEGEND! HE'S THE HUDSON HORNET. HE WON THREE PISTON CUPS!
I'VE NEVER SEEN DOC DRIVE MORE THAN TWENTY MILES AN HOUR. I MEAN, HAVE YOU EVER SEEN HIM RACE?
No matter how hard he tries, McQueen can't convince them.
WHAT'S THE KID TALKING ABOUT?
KID'S GOTTA SCREW LOOSE.
DUDE'S HALLUCINATING, MAN.

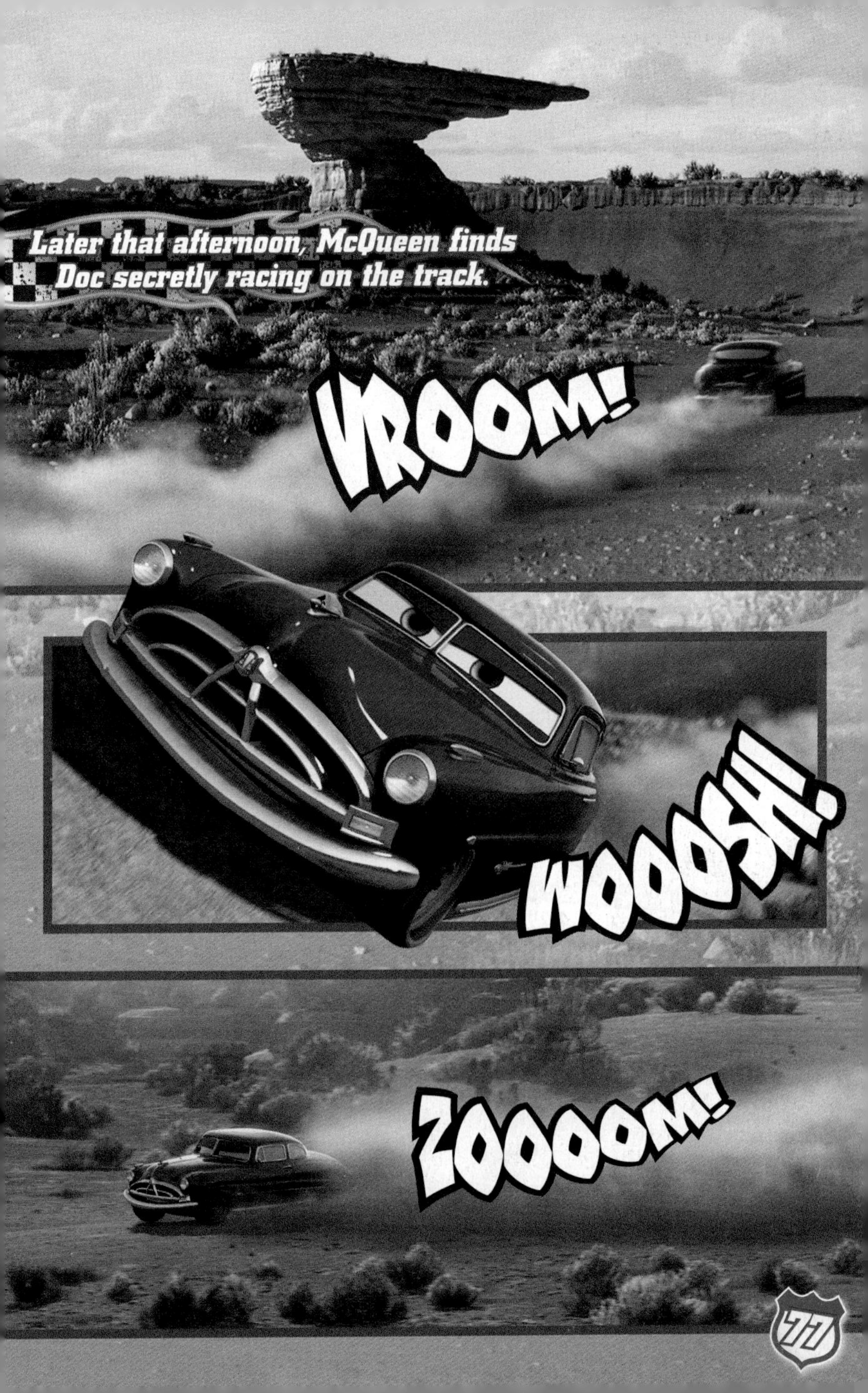
Later that afternoon, McQueen finds Doc secretly racing on the track.
VROOM!
WOOOSH!
ZOOOOM!

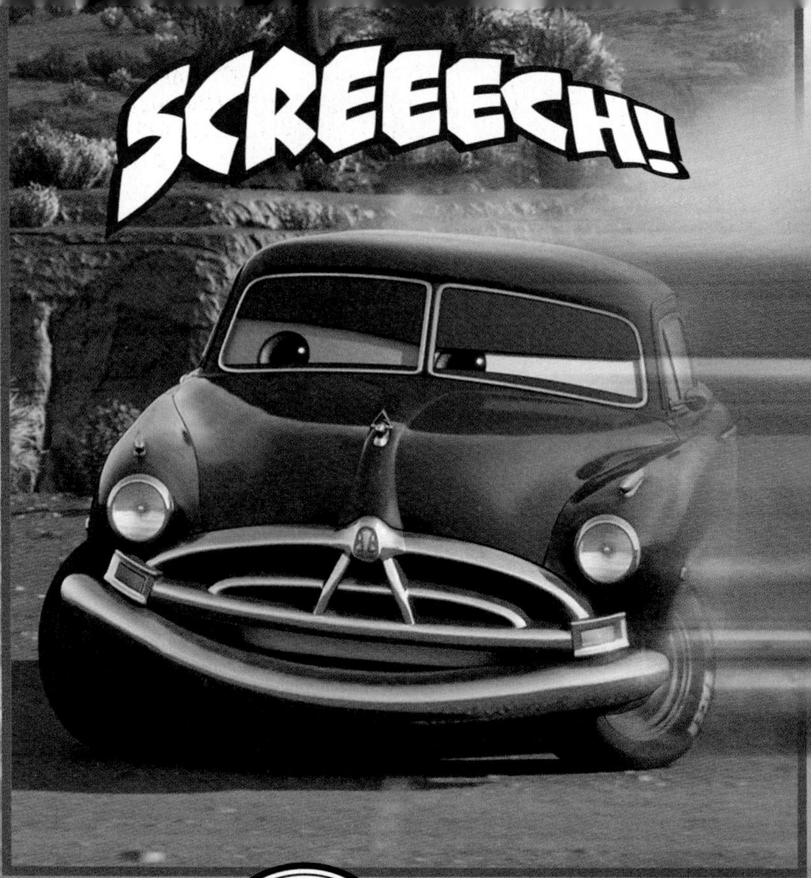
SCREEECH!

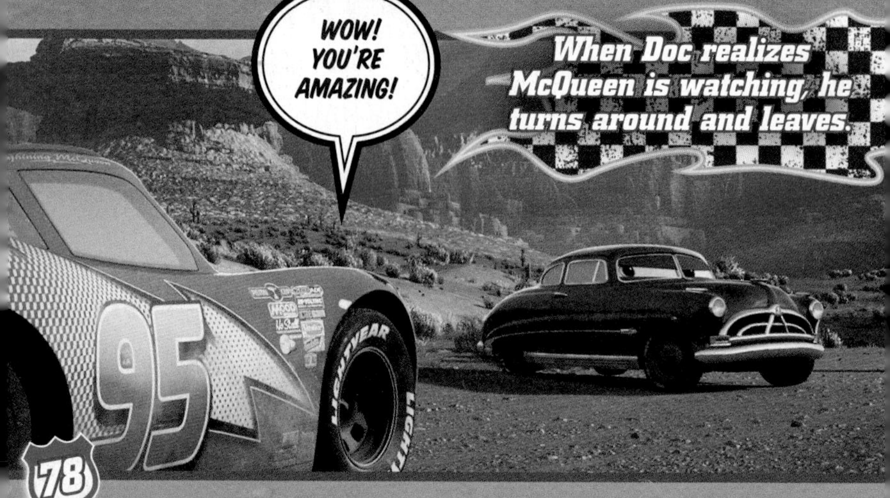
WOW! YOU'RE AMAZING!
When Doc realizes McQueen is watching, he turns around and leaves.

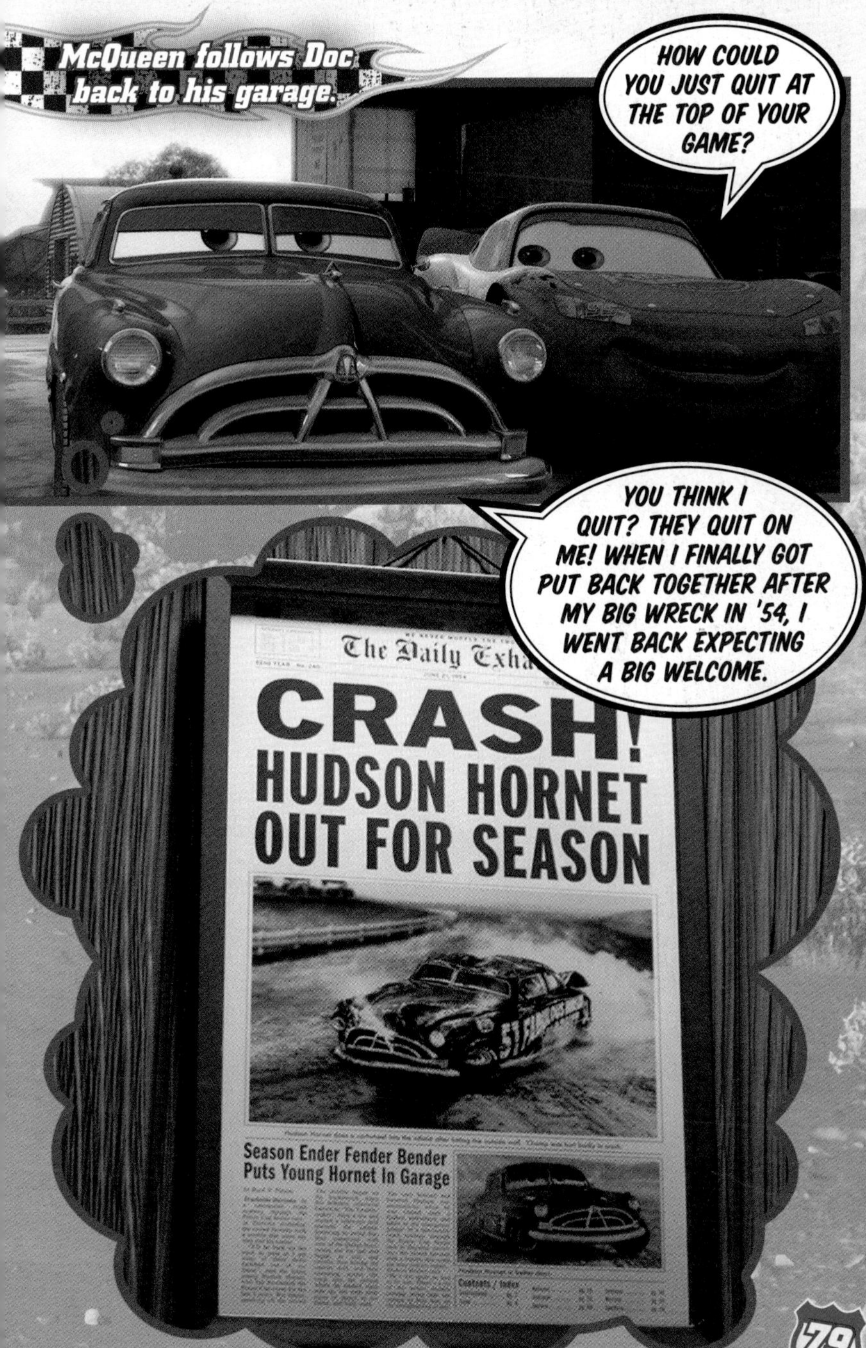
McQueen follows Doc back to his garage.
HOW COULD YOU JUST QUIT AT THE TOP OF YOUR GAME?
YOU THINK I QUIT? THEY QUIT ON ME! WHEN I FINALLY GOT PUT BACK TOGETHER AFTER MY BIG WRECK IN '54, I WENT BACK EXPECTING A BIG WELCOME.
The Daily Exha
CRASH!
HUDSON HORNET OUT FOR SEASON
Season Ender Fender Bender Puts Young Hornet In Garage
Contents / Index

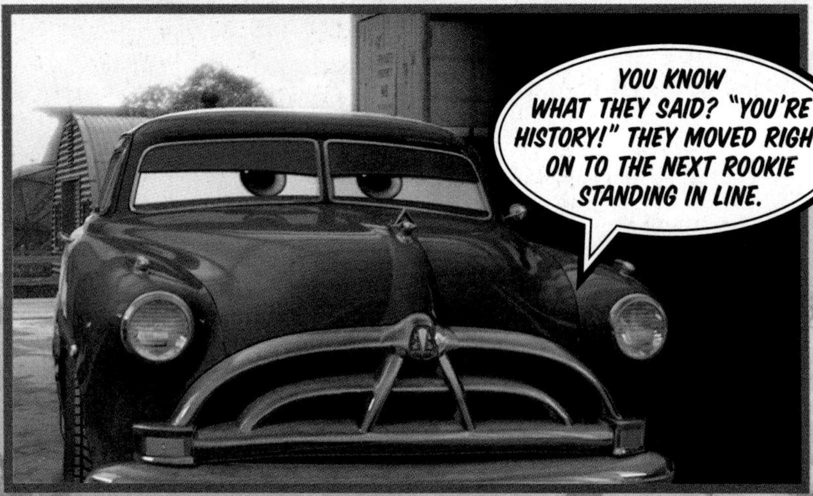
YOU KNOW WHAT THEY SAID? "YOU'RE HISTORY!" THEY MOVED RIGHT ON TO THE NEXT ROOKIE STANDING IN LINE.

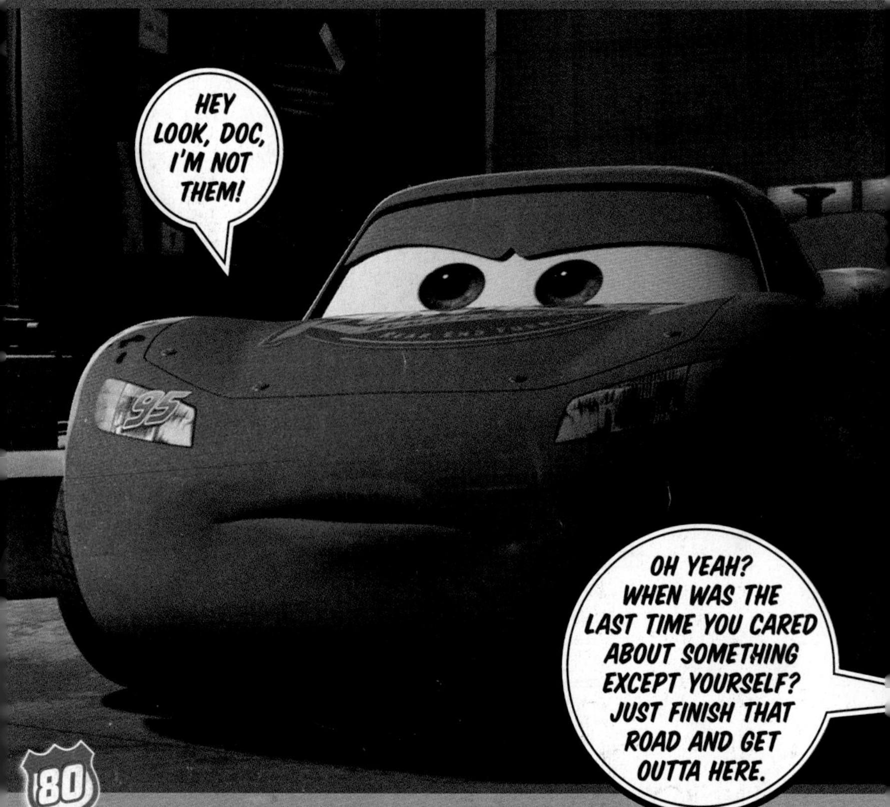
HEY LOOK, DOC, I'M NOT THEM!
OH YEAH? WHEN WAS THE LAST TIME YOU CARED ABOUT SOMETHING EXCEPT YOURSELF? JUST FINISH THAT ROAD AND GET OUTTA HERE.

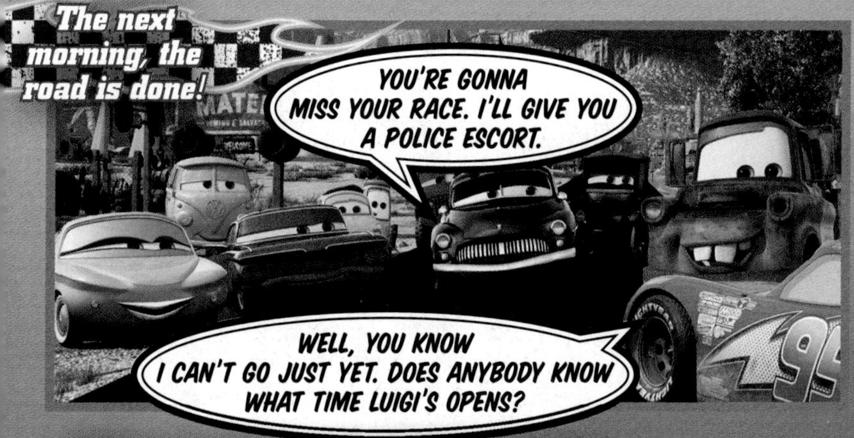
The next morning, the road is done!
YOU'RE GONNA MISS YOUR RACE. I'LL GIVE YOU A POLICE ESCORT.
WELL, YOU KNOW I CAN'T GO JUST YET. DOES ANYBODY KNOW WHAT TIME LUIGI'S OPENS?

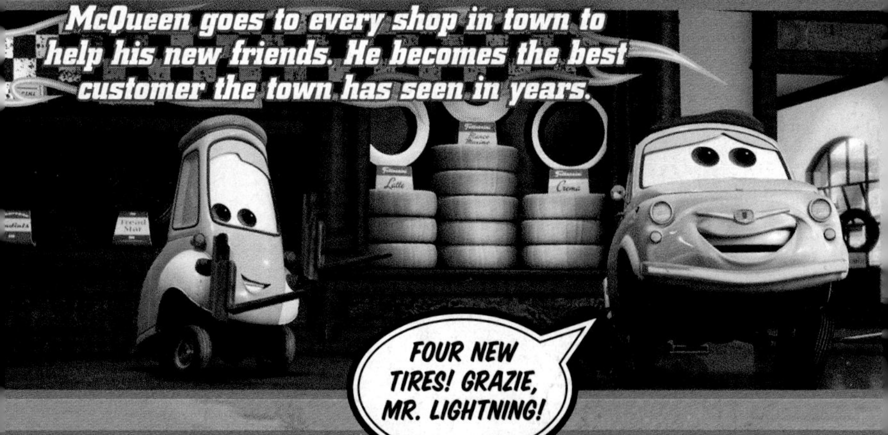
McQueen goes to every shop in town to help his new friends. He becomes the best customer the town has seen in years.
FOUR NEW TIRES! GRAZIE, MR. LIGHTNING!

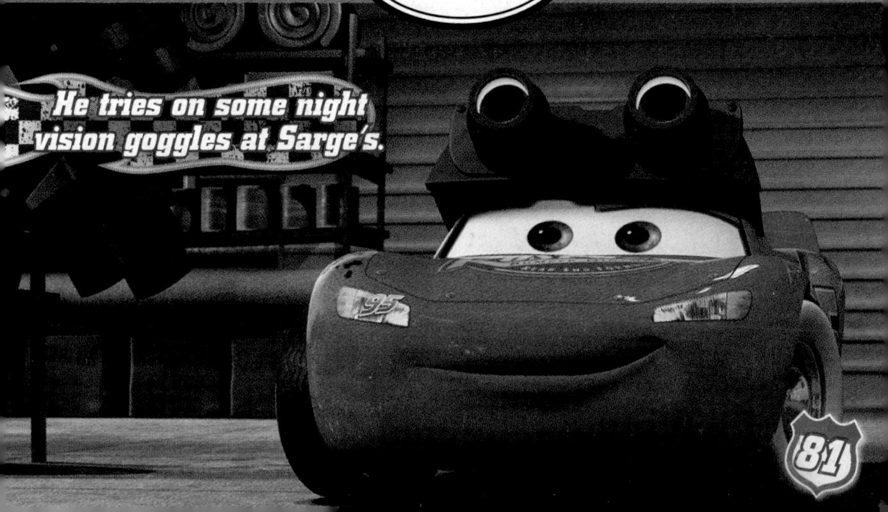
He tries on some night vision goggles at Sarge's.

And Ramone gives him a new paint job. Lightning McQueen looks like a new car!

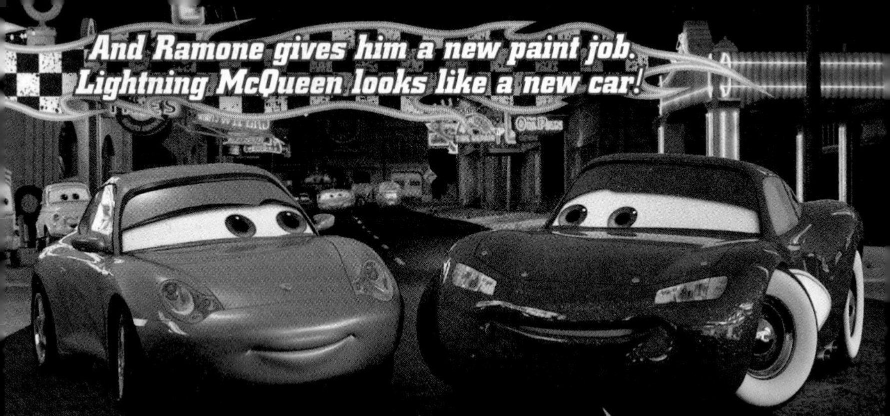

That night everyone happily cruises down the street under the glow of the newly repaired neon signs. The town is just like in its heyday.

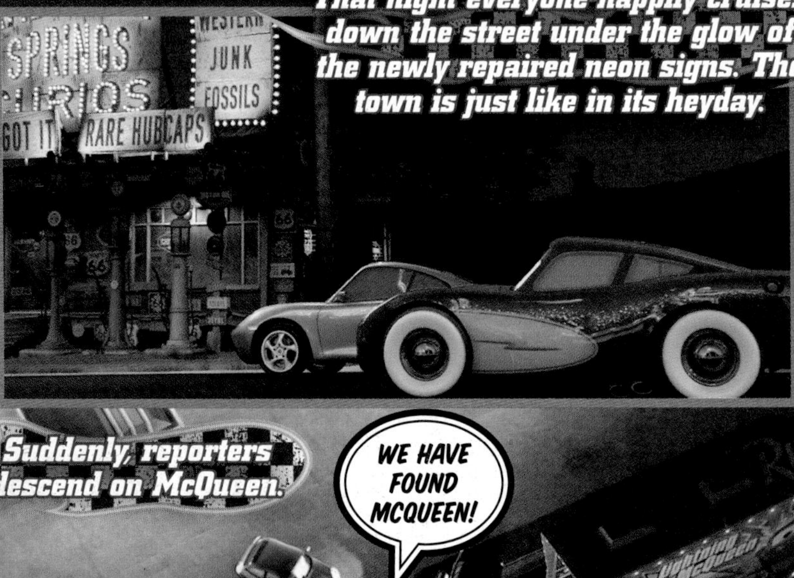
SPRINGS
CURIOS
WESTERN
JUNK
FOSSILS
GOT IT
RARE HUBCAPS

Suddenly, reporters descend on McQueen.

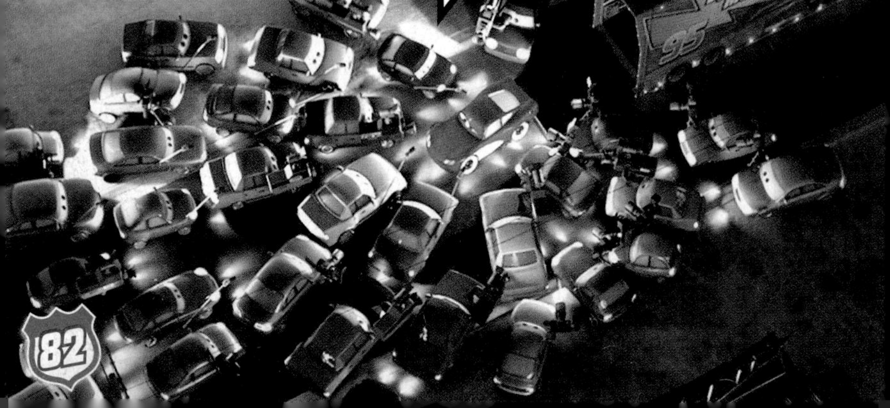
WE HAVE FOUND MCQUEEN!

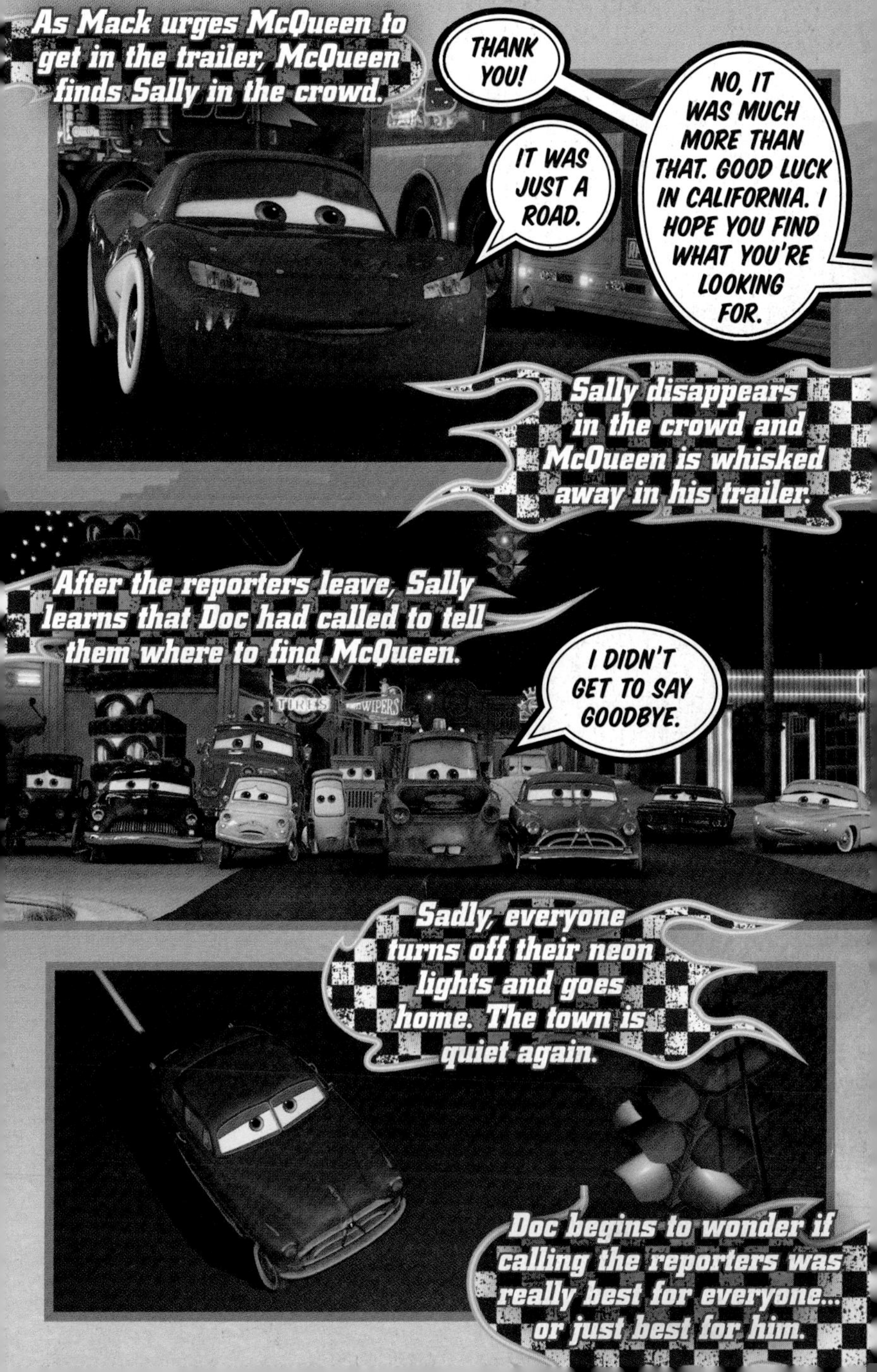

As Mack urges McQueen to get in the trailer, McQueen finds Sally in the crowd.
THANK YOU!
IT WAS JUST A ROAD.
NO, IT WAS MUCH MORE THAN THAT. GOOD LUCK IN CALIFORNIA. I HOPE YOU FIND WHAT YOU'RE LOOKING FOR.
Sally disappears in the crowd and McQueen is whisked away in his trailer.
After the reporters leave, Sally learns that Doc had called to tell them where to find McQueen.
I DIDN'T GET TO SAY GOODBYE.
Sadly, everyone turns off their neon lights and goes home. The town is quiet again.
Doc begins to wonder if calling the reporters was really best for everyone... or just best for him.

At the Piston Cup...

LOS ANGELES INTERNATIONAL SPEEDWAY

PISTON CUP

...the race begins!

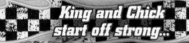

King and Chick start off strong...

OFFICIAL

PISTON

UUUUGH! SHOOT!

43

VROOM!

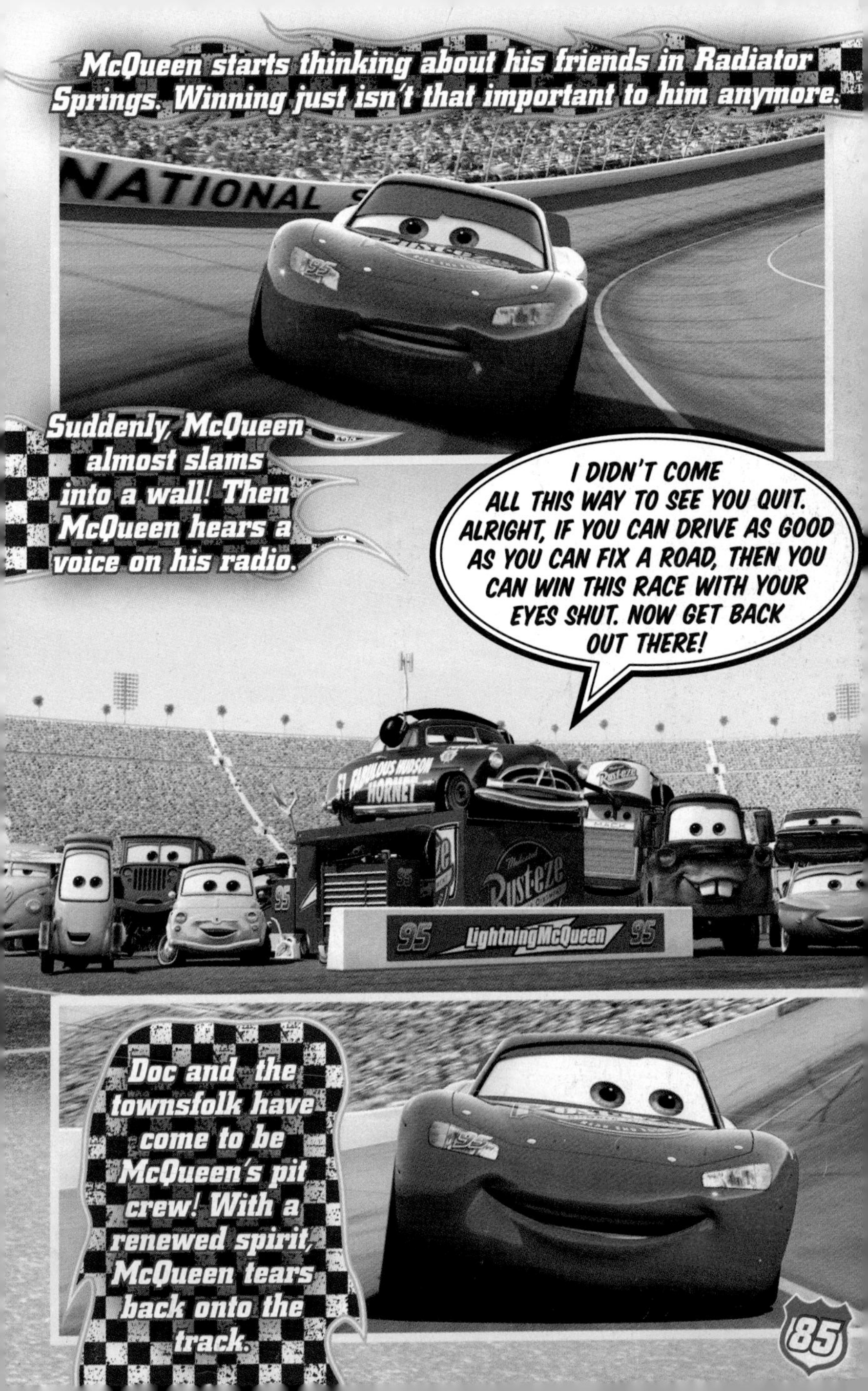
McQueen starts thinking about his friends in Radiator Springs. Winning just isn't that important to him anymore.
NATIONAL
Suddenly, McQueen almost slams into a wall! Then McQueen hears a voice on his radio.
I DIDN'T COME ALL THIS WAY TO SEE YOU QUIT. ALRIGHT, IF YOU CAN DRIVE AS GOOD AS YOU CAN FIX A ROAD, THEN YOU CAN WIN THIS RACE WITH YOUR EYES SHUT. NOW GET BACK OUT THERE!
51 FABULOUS HUDSON HORNET
95 LightningMcQueen 95
Rust-eze
Doc and the townsfolk have come to be McQueen's pit crew! With a renewed spirit, McQueen tears back onto the track.

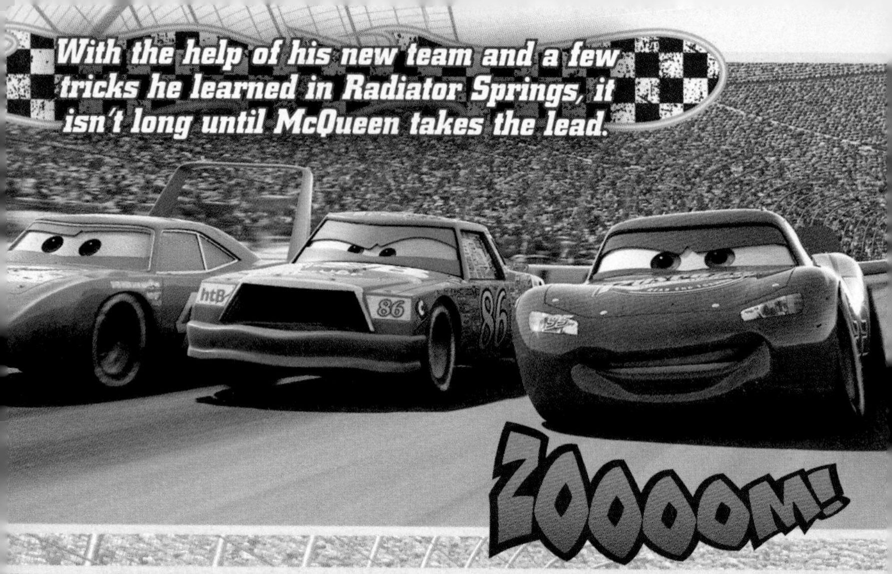
With the help of his new team and a few tricks he learned in Radiator Springs, it isn't long until McQueen takes the lead.
ZOOOOM!

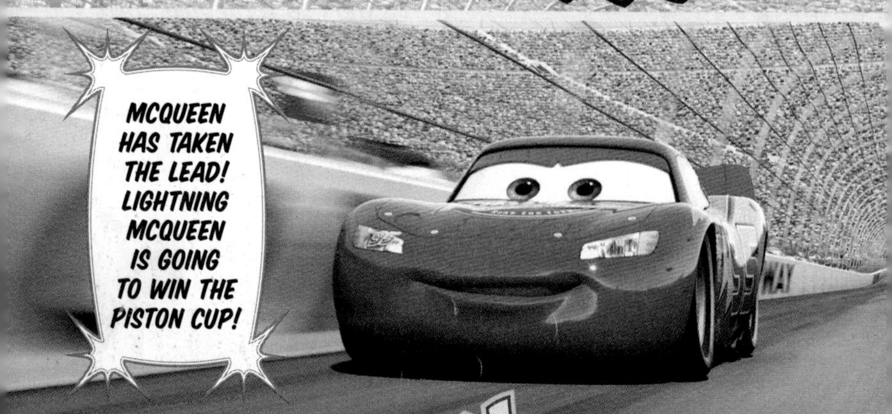
MCQUEEN HAS TAKEN THE LEAD! LIGHTNING MCQUEEN IS GOING TO WIN THE PISTON CUP!

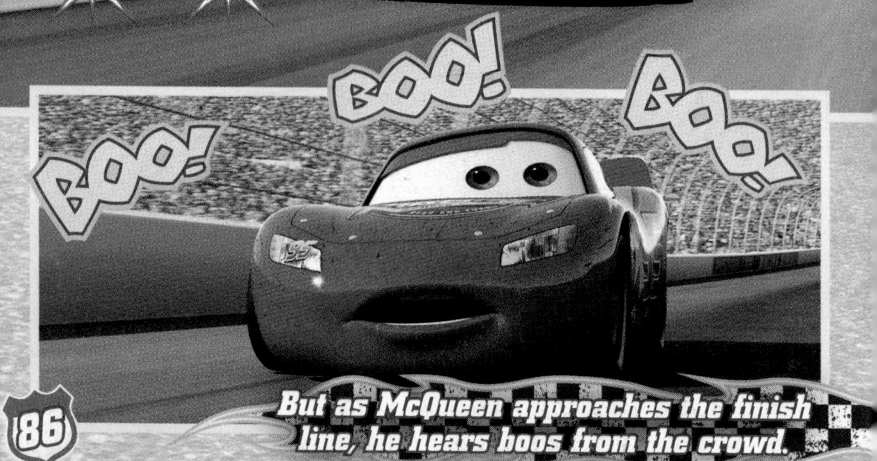
BOO!
BOO!
BOO!
But as McQueen approaches the finish line, he hears boos from the crowd.

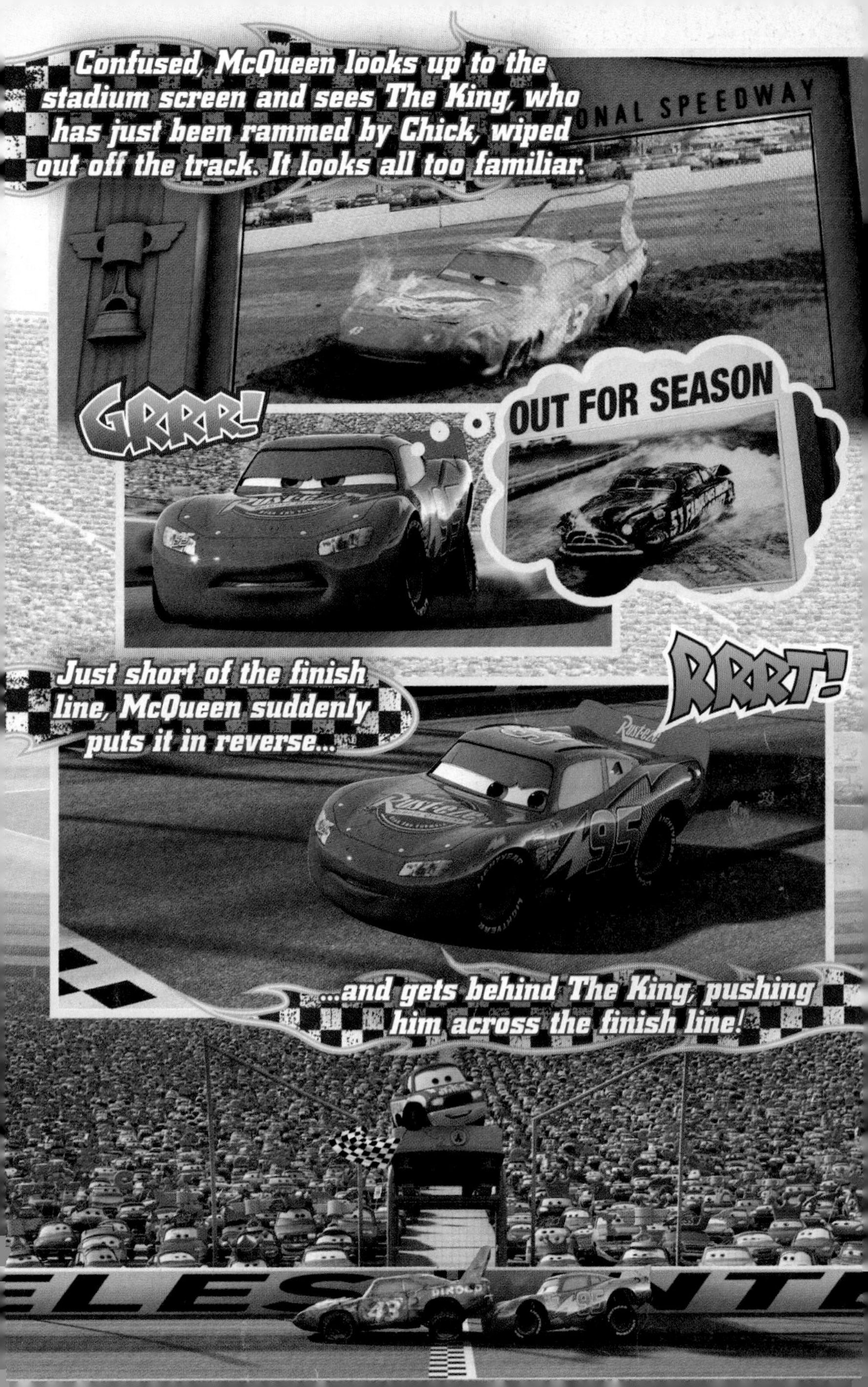
Confused, McQueen looks up to the stadium screen and sees The King, who has just been rammed by Chick, wiped out off the track. It looks all too familiar.
ONAL SPEEDWAY
GRRR!
OUT FOR SEASON
Just short of the finish line, McQueen suddenly puts it in reverse...
RRRT!
...and gets behind The King, pushing him across the finish line!

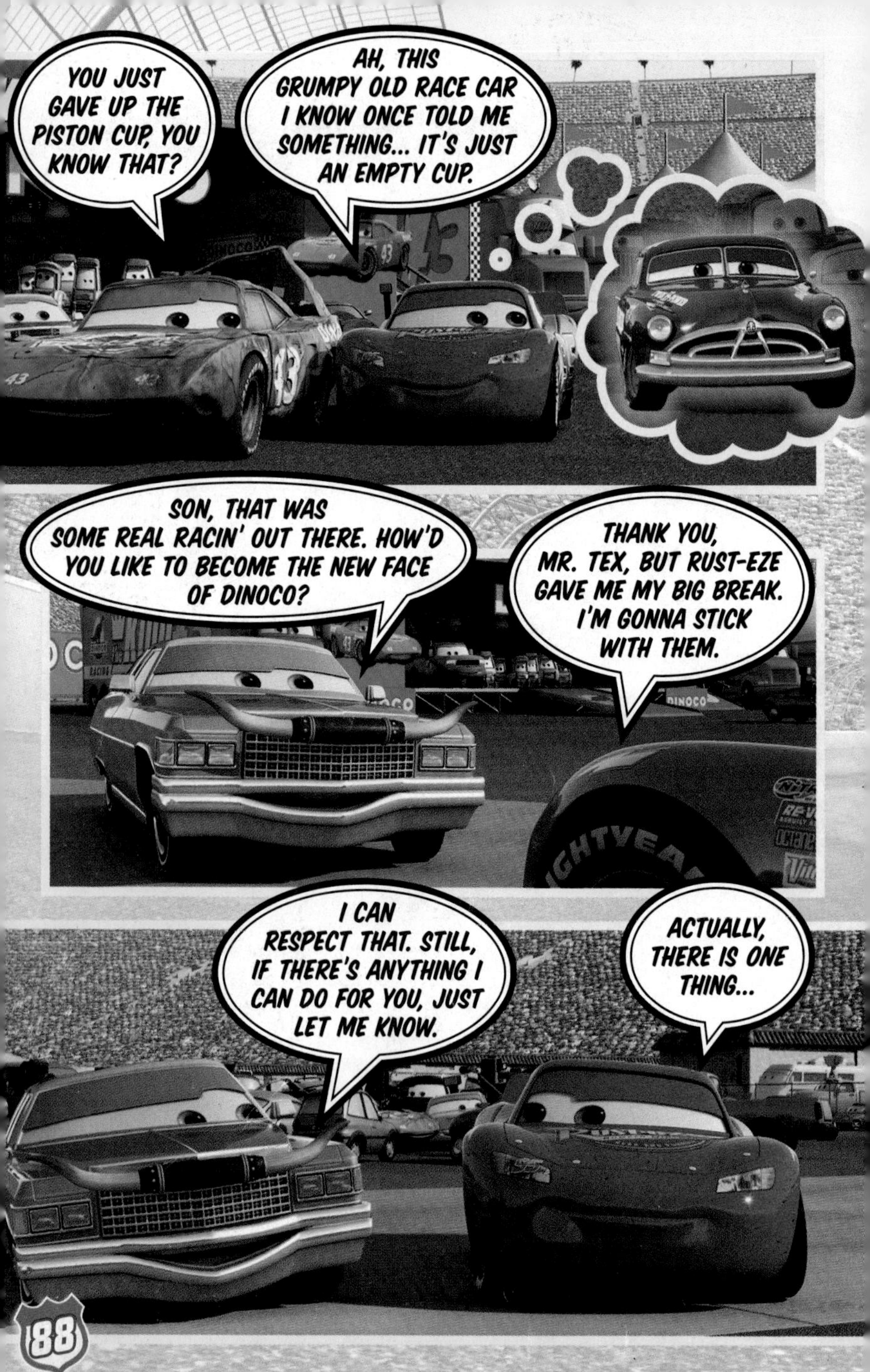
YOU JUST GAVE UP THE PISTON CUP, YOU KNOW THAT?
AH, THIS GRUMPY OLD RACE CAR I KNOW ONCE TOLD ME SOMETHING... IT'S JUST AN EMPTY CUP.
SON, THAT WAS SOME REAL RACIN' OUT THERE. HOW'D YOU LIKE TO BECOME THE NEW FACE OF DINOCO?
THANK YOU, MR. TEX, BUT RUST-EZE GAVE ME MY BIG BREAK. I'M GONNA STICK WITH THEM.
I CAN RESPECT THAT. STILL, IF THERE'S ANYTHING I CAN DO FOR YOU, JUST LET ME KNOW.
ACTUALLY, THERE IS ONE THING...

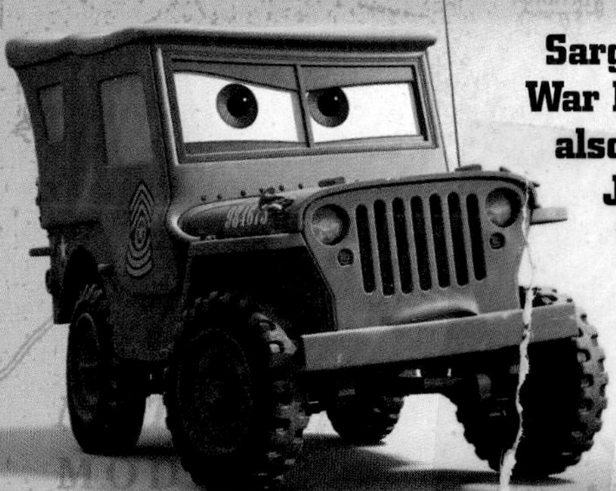

Sarge is a 1942 World War II Willys Army Jeep, also known as the Willys Jeep, GI Jeep, World War II Jeep, or just plain Army Jeep. This model saw lots of action in World War II.

Fillmore is a 1960 Volkswagen Bus. Volkswagen means "the people's car" in German, which makes sense, since Volkswagen made inexpensive cars that anyone could afford. During the late '60s and early '70s, the Bus was considered the car of the hippie.

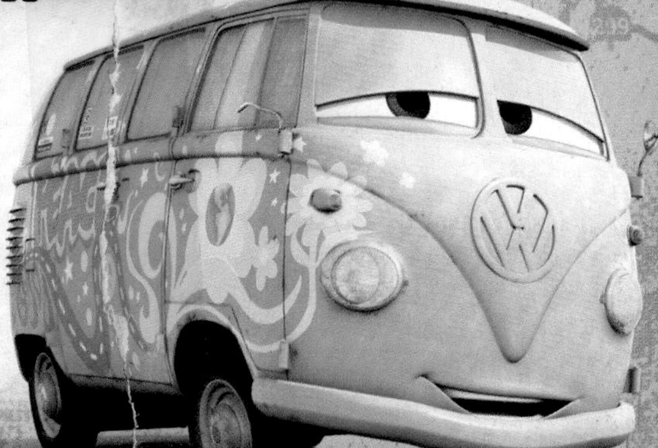

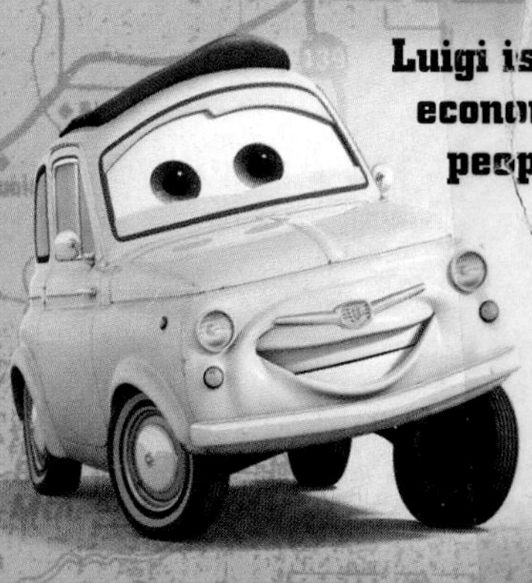

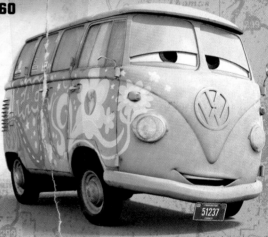

Luigi is a 1959 Fiat 500, a tiny economy car that could fit four people, just not their luggage. Due to the Fiat 500's size, some models came with roof racks for added storage—though others came with a large sunroof like Luigi's instead.

DISNEY PRESENTS A PIXAR FILM

Cars

Video Game Available June 2006

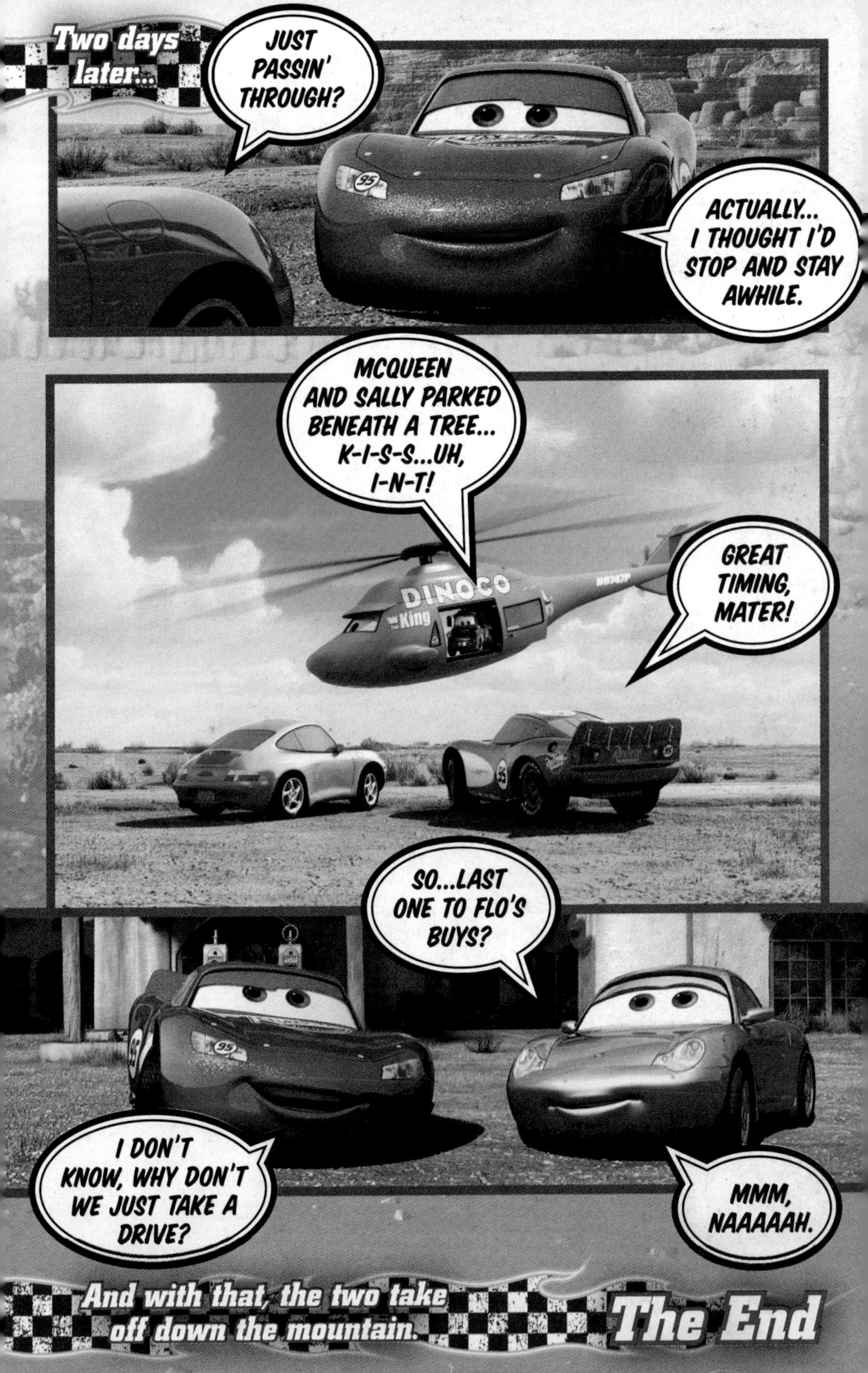
Two days later...
JUST PASSIN' THROUGH?
ACTUALLY... I THOUGHT I'D STOP AND STAY AWHILE.
MCQUEEN AND SALLY PARKED BENEATH A TREE... K-I-S-S...UH, I-N-T!
DINOCO
GREAT TIMING, MATER!
SO...LAST ONE TO FLO'S BUYS?
I DON'T KNOW, WHY DON'T WE JUST TAKE A DRIVE?
MMM, NAAAAAH.
And with that, the two take off down the mountain.
The End

Ramone is a 1959 two-door hardtop Impala. This '59 model is often referred to as bat-winged because of the rear styling. Some Impalas have hydraulics installed that allow the car to drive on three wheels, allowing the front end to bounce up and down or the entire car to lift.

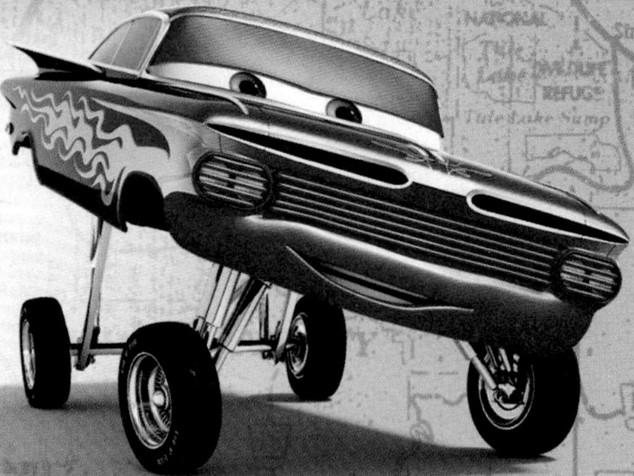

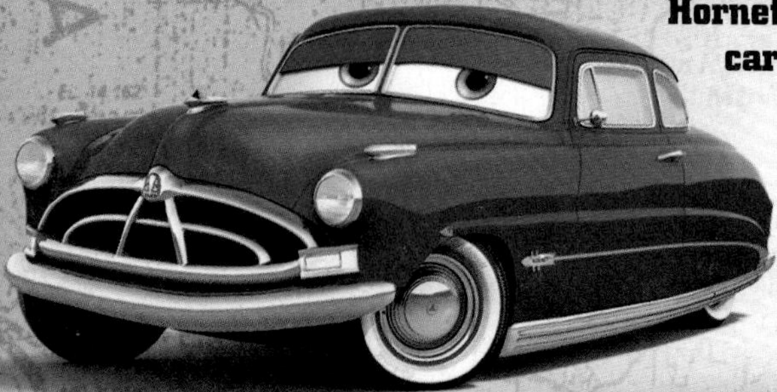

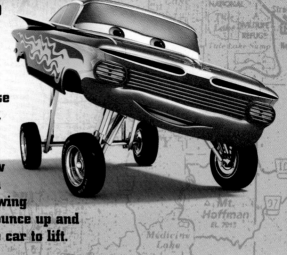

Doc Hudson is a 1951 Hudson Hornet. This popular stock car did actually race on the NASCAR circuit the year the Hornet came out and won the Grand National race many times over.

This model featured an extra-high rear wing and a pointed nose. The Superbird with the 426 Hemi engine is considered by some to be the most valuable muscle car ever made. It was designed for NASCAR, but was also available to the public. This car was only made in 1970.

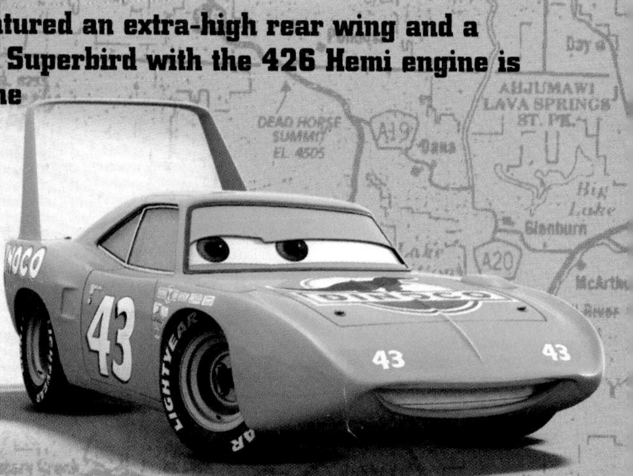
43
43
43